From Genesis to Revelation

Seven Scriptural Rosaries

Christine Haapala

Christendom Press
Front Royal, Virginia

**This book is dedicated
to the Blessed Virgin Mary,
the Immaculate Conception.**

Special thanks to Father Michael Duesterhaus
for his spiritual direction and encouragement.

Special appreciation to Christine Parson
for her religious *duplettes*.

Loving gratitude to my husband, Kenneth,
for his constant support.

This book could not have been envisioned were it not for
the religious seeds sown by years of Catholic education
made possible by the self-sacrifice of my parents, Alice
and Norman Walecka.

Published with Ecclesiastical Permission
Diocese of Arlington
July 10, 1995

Cover illustration: "Woman" (Genesis 3:15, John 19:26)
by Christine Parson.

Table of Contents

From Genesis to Revelation

Seven Scriptural Rosaries

First Born ... Pierced with a Sword

Genesis 22:6; Exodus 13:1-2; Luke 2:35; John 19:34

BOOK ONE
The Pentateuch

His care is to seek the LORD, his Maker, to petition the Most High, To open his lips in prayer, to ask pardon for his sins ... He will pour forth his words of wisdom and in prayer give thanks to the LORD, Who will direct his knowledge and his counsel, as he meditates upon his mysteries. *Sirach 39:6-7*

The Our Father Meditation Verses

Selections from Exodus

The Hail Mary Meditation Verses

Selections from Baruch, Deuteronomy, Exodus, Genesis, Judith, Leviticus, 1 Maccabees, 2 Maccabees, Numbers, Sirach, Tobit, Wisdom

The Joyful Mysteries

The Sign of the Cross

The Apostle's Creed

"See, I am sending an angel before you, to guard you on the way and bring you to the place I have prepared. Be attentive to him and heed his voice." *Exodus 23:20-21*

Our Father...

The LORD also told him, "I am coming to you in a dense cloud, so that when the people hear me speaking with you, they may always have faith in you also."
Exodus 19:9

Hail Mary for Faith

Your deed of hope will never be forgotten by those who tell of the might of God. *Judith 13:19*

Hail Mary for Hope

Happy are those who love you, and happy those who rejoice in your prosperity. *Tobit 13:14*

Hail Mary for Charity

Glory Be to the Father...

O My Jesus...

First Joyful Mystery
Annunciation

My strength and my courage is the LORD, and he has been my savior. *Exodus 15:2*

Our Father...

The LORD God formed man out of the clay of the ground and blew into his nostrils the breath of life, and so man became a living being. *Genesis 2:7*

Hail Mary...

God created man in his image; in the divine image he created him; male and female he created them.
Genesis 1:27

Hail Mary...

Before all ages, in the beginning, he created me, and through all ages I shall not cease to be. *Sirach 24:9*

Hail Mary...

When God, in the beginning, created man, he made him subject to his own free choice. If you choose you can keep the commandments, it is loyalty to do his will.
Sirach 15:14-15

Hail Mary...

"Hear, O Israel! The LORD is our God, the LORD alone! Therefore, you shall love the LORD, your God, with all your heart, and with all your soul, and with all your strength." *Deuteronomy 6:4-5*

Hail Mary...

But to those who fear you, you are very merciful.
Judith 16:15

Hail Mary...

The beginning of wisdom is fear of the Lord, which is
formed with the faithful in the womb. *Sirach 1:12*

Hail Mary...

For fear of the LORD is wisdom and culture; loyal
humility is his delight. *Sirach 1:24*

Hail Mary...

Your handmaid is, indeed, a God-fearing woman,
serving the God of heaven night and day. *Judith 11:17*

Hail Mary...

"I will put enmity between you and the woman, and
between your offspring and hers; he will strike at your
head, while you strike at his heel." *Genesis 3:15*

Hail Mary...

Glory Be to the Father...

O My Jesus...

Second Joyful Mystery
Visitation

"The God of the Hebrews has sent us word. Let us go a three days' journey in the desert, that we may offer sacrifice to the LORD our God..." *Exodus 5:3*

Our Father...

O Lord GOD, you have begun to show to your servant your greatness and might. *Deuteronomy 3:24*

Hail Mary...

"I am God the Almighty. Walk in my presence and be blameless." *Genesis 17:1*

Hail Mary...

"Keep the commandments of the LORD, your God, by walking in his ways and fearing him. For the LORD, your God, is bringing you into a good country..."
Deuteronomy 8:6-7

Hail Mary...

And now, bless the God of all, who has done wondrous things on earth; who fosters men's growth from their mother's womb, and fashions them according to his will!
Sirach 50:22
Hail Mary...

"May you be blessed in the city, and blessed in the country! Blessed be the fruit of your womb..."
Deuteronomy 28:3-4

Hail Mary...

But the LORD said to Abraham: "Why did Sarah laugh and say, 'Shall I really bear a child, old as I am?' Is anything too marvelous for the LORD to do?" *Genesis 18:13-14*

Hail Mary...

The LORD, your God, has blessed you in all your undertakings; he has been concerned about your journey through this vast desert. *Deuteronomy 2:7*

Hail Mary...

"A prophet like me will the LORD, your God, raise up for you from among your own kinsmen; to him you shall listen." *Deuteronomy 18:15*

Hail Mary...

Is this beyond the LORD's reach? You shall see now whether or not what I have promised you takes place. *Numbers 11:23*

Hail Mary...

God replied: "Nevertheless, your wife Sarah is to bear you a son, and you shall call him Isaac. I will maintain my covenant with him as an everlasting pact, to be his God and the God of his descendants after him." *Genesis 17:19*

Hail Mary...

Glory Be to the Father...

O My Jesus...

Third Joyful Mystery
Nativity

From every man you shall accept the contribution that
his heart prompts him to give me. These are ... gold ...
spices for the anointing oil and for the fragrant incense...
Exodus 25:2-3,6

Our Father...

"Take a census of the whole community of the Israelites,
by clans and ancestral houses, registering each male
individually." *Numbers 1:2*

Hail Mary...

Do not be discouraged, my child, because of our
poverty. You will be a rich man if you fear God, avoid
all sin, and do what is right before the Lord your God.
Tobit 4:21

Hail Mary...

For even his covenant with David, the son of Jesse of the
tribe of Judah, was an individual heritage through one
son alone; but the heritage of Aaron is for all his
descendants. *Sirach 45:25*

Hail Mary...

David, for his piety, received as a heritage a throne of
everlasting royalty. *1 Maccabees 2:57*

Hail Mary...

"I will make of you a great nation, and I will bless you; I will make your name great, so that you will be a blessing." *Genesis 12:2*

Hail Mary...

"I will bless those who bless you ... All the communities of the earth shall find blessing in you." *Genesis 12:3*

Hail Mary...

Joy and gladness he will find, an everlasting name inherit. *Sirach 15:6*

Hail Mary...

"Remove the sandals from your feet, for the place where you stand is holy ground. I am ... the God of Abraham, the God of Isaac, the God of Jacob." *Exodus 3:5*

Hail Mary...

God acknowledged him as the first-born, and gave him his inheritance. *Sirach 44:23*

Hail Mary...

In swaddling clothes and with constant care I was nurtured. *Wisdom 7:4*

Hail Mary...

Glory Be to the Father...

O My Jesus...

Fourth Joyful Mystery
Presentation

The LORD spoke to Moses and said, "Consecrate to me every first-born..." *Exodus 13:1-2*

Our Father...

Reflect on the precepts of the LORD, let his commandments be your constant meditation; then he will enlighten your mind, and the wisdom you desire he will grant. *Sirach 6:37*

Hail Mary...

All wisdom is fear of the LORD; perfect wisdom is the fulfillment of the law. *Sirach 19:17*

Hail Mary...

Study the generations long past and understand; has anyone hoped in the LORD and been disappointed? *Sirach 2:10*

Hail Mary...

"Observe my precepts and be careful to keep my regulations, for then you will dwell securely in the land." *Leviticus 25:18*

Hail Mary...

"Love the LORD, your God, therefore, and always heed his charge: his statutes, decrees and commandments." *Deuteronomy 11:1*

Hail Mary...

Throughout the ages, every male among you, when he is eight days old, shall be circumcised... *Genesis 17:12*

Hail Mary...

God also said to Abraham "On your part, you and your descendants after you must keep my covenant throughout the ages..." *Genesis 17:9*

Hail Mary...

Honor God and respect the priest; give him his portion as you have been commanded: First fruits and contributions, due sacrifices and holy offerings. *Sirach 7:31*

Hail Mary...

"Through all your days, my son, keep the Lord in mind, and suppress every desire to sin or to break his commandments. Perform good works all the days of your life..." *Tobit 4:5*

Hail Mary...

Let all men speak of his majesty, and sing his praises in Jerusalem. *Tobit 13:8*

Hail Mary...

Glory Be to the Father...

O My Jesus...

Fifth Joyful Mystery
Finding in the Temple

"Honor your father and your mother..." *Exodus 20:12*

Our Father...

For I am your servant, the son of your handmaid...
Wisdom 9:5

Hail Mary...

He professes to have knowledge of God and styles
himself as a child of the LORD. *Wisdom 2:13*

Hail Mary...

I beg you, child, to look at the heavens and the earth and
see all that is in them; then you will know that God did
not make them out of existing things; and in the same
way the human race came into existence.
2 Maccabees 7:28

Hail Mary...

This is the priestly share from the oblations of the LORD,
allotted to Aaron and his sons on the day he called them
to be the priests of the LORD... *Leviticus 7:35*

Hail Mary...

"Assemble and listen, sons of Jacob, listen to Israel, your
father." *Genesis 49:2*

Hail Mary...

O Israel, how vast is the house of God, how broad the scope of his dominion: vast and endless, high and immeasurable! *Baruch 3:24-25*

Hail Mary...

He calls blest the destiny of the just and boasts that God is his Father. *Wisdom 2:16*

Hail Mary...

Give new signs and work new wonders; show forth the splendor of your right hand and arm... *Sirach 36:5*

Hail Mary...

Peoples will speak of his wisdom, and in assembly sing his praises. *Sirach 39:10*

Hail Mary...

Blessed be God, and praised be his great name, and blessed be all his holy angels. May his holy name be praised throughout all the ages. *Tobit 11:14*

Hail Mary...

Glory Be to the Father...

O My Jesus...

Hail Holy Queen...

The Sorrowful Mysteries

The Sign of the Cross

The Apostle's Creed

Still the Israelites groaned and cried out because of their slavery. As their cry for release went up to God, he heard their groaning and was mindful of his covenant with Abraham, Isaac and Jacob. *Exodus 2:23-24*

Our Father...

Hananiah, Azariah and Mishael, for their faith, were saved from the fire. *1 Maccabees 2:59*

Hail Mary for Faith

Woe to you who have lost hope! *Sirach 2:14*

Hail Mary for Hope

You shall win great glory and an everlasting name. *1 Maccabees 2:51*

Hail Mary for Charity

Glory Be to the Father...

O My Jesus...

First Sorrowful Mystery
Agony in the Garden

"Fear not! Stand your ground, and you will see the victory the LORD will win for you today." *Exodus 14:13*

Our Father...

"Please, please, God of my forefather, God of the heritage of Israel, LORD of heaven and earth, Creator of the waters, King of all you have created, hear my prayer!" *Judith 9:12*

Hail Mary...

I will ever praise your name and be constant in my prayers to you. *Sirach 51:11*

Hail Mary...

O LORD, look down from your holy dwelling and take thought of us; turn, O LORD, your ear to hear us.
Baruch 2:16

Hail Mary...

Therefore I prayed, and prudence was given me; I pleaded, and the spirit of Wisdom came to me.
Wisdom 7:7

Hail Mary...

Hear, O LORD, our prayer of supplication, and deliver us for your own sake: grant us favor in the presence of our captors, that the whole earth may know that you are the LORD, our God... *Baruch 2:14-15*

Hail Mary...

You are righteous, O Lord, and all your deeds are just;
All your ways are mercy and truth; you are the judge of
the world. *Tobit 3:2*

Hail Mary...

Fear not death's decree for you; remember, it embraces
those before you, and those after. Thus God has
ordained for all flesh; why then should you reject the
will of the Most High? *Sirach 41:3-4*

Hail Mary...

My son, hold fast to your duty, busy yourself with it.
Sirach 11:20

Hail Mary...

Lord, command me to be delivered from such anguish;
let me go to the everlasting abode; Lord refuse me not.
Tobit 3:6

Hail Mary...

[He] stretched forth his hand for the cup, to offer blood
of the grape, And poured it out at the foot of the altar, a
sweet-smelling odor to the Most High God. *Sirach 50:15*

Hail Mary...

Glory Be to the Father...

O My Jesus...

Second Sorrowful Mystery
Scourging

"This is the blood of the covenant which the LORD has made with you..." *Exodus 24:8*

Our Father...

Accept whatever befalls you, in crushing misfortune be patient. *Sirach 2:4*

Hail Mary...

A patient man need stand firm but for a time, and then contentment comes back to him. *Sirach 1:20*

Hail Mary...

No evil can harm the man who fears the LORD; through trials, again and again he is safe. *Sirach 33:1*

Hail Mary...

Forty stripes may be given him, but no more; lest, if he were beaten with more stripes than these, your kinsman should be looked upon as disgraced because of the severity of the beating. *Deuteronomy 25:3*

Hail Mary...

The LORD in his holy knowledge knows full well that, although I could have escaped death, I am not only enduring terrible pain in my body from this scourging, but also suffering it with joy in my soul because of my devotion to him. *2 Maccabees 6:30*

Hail Mary...

From man in regard to his fellow man I will demand an accounting for human life. *Genesis 9:5*

Hail Mary...

The LORD has commanded that what has been done today be done to make atonement for you.
Leviticus 8:34

Hail Mary...

For he scourges and then has mercy; he casts down to the depths of the nether world, and he brings up from the great abyss. *Tobit 13:2*

Hail Mary...

Close at hand is the day of their disaster, and their doom is rushing upon them! *Deuteronomy 32:35*

Hail Mary...

So you handed us over to plundering, exile, and death... *Tobit 3:4*

Hail Mary...

Glory Be to the Father...

O My Jesus...

Third Sorrowful Mystery
Crowning with Thorns

"I am who am." *Exodus 3:14*

Our Father...

You are the God of the lowly, the helper of the oppressed, the supporter of the weak, the protector of the forsaken, the savior of those without hope.
Judith 9:11

Hail Mary...

My son, when you come to serve the LORD, prepare yourself for trials. *Sirach 2:1*

Hail Mary...

If anyone sheds the blood of man, by man shall his blood be shed; For in the image of God has man been made. *Genesis 9:6*

Hail Mary...

"How long will this wicked community grumble against me? I have heard the grumblings of the Israelites against me." *Numbers 14:27*

Hail Mary...

With revilement and torture let us put him to the test that we may have proof of his gentleness and try his patience. *Wisdom 2:19*

Hail Mary...

Even to the death fight for truth, and the LORD your God will battle for you. *Sirach 4:28*

Hail Mary...

Those who trust in him shall understand truth...
Wisdom 3:9

Hail Mary...

Seek not from the LORD authority, nor from the king a place of honor. Parade not your justice before the LORD, and before the king flaunt not your wisdom. *Sirach 7:4-5*

Hail Mary...

For if before men, indeed, they be punished, yet is their hope full of immortality; Chastised a little, they shall be greatly blessed, because God tried them and found them worthy of himself. *Wisdom 3:4-5*

Hail Mary...

It is my choice to die at the hands of men with the God-given hope of being restored to life by him.
2 Maccabees 7:14

Hail Mary...

Glory Be to the Father...

O My Jesus...

Fourth Sorrowful Mystery
Carrying of the Cross

Moses again had recourse to the LORD and said, "Lord, why do you treat this people so badly? And why did you send me on such a mission?" *Exodus 5:22*

Our Father...

Most important of all, pray to God to set your feet in the path of truth. *Sirach 37:15*

Hail Mary...

The LORD, your God, shall you follow, and him shall you fear; his commandment shall you observe, and his voice shall you heed, serving him and holding fast to him alone. *Deuteronomy 13:5*

Hail Mary...

Work at your tasks in due season, and in his own time God will give you your reward. *Sirach 51:30*

Hail Mary...

"Be brave and steadfast; have no fear or dread of them, for it is the LORD, your God, who marches with you; he will never fail you or forsake you." *Deuteronomy 31:6*

Hail Mary...

Consider this from generation to generation, that none who hope in him shall fail in strength. *1 Maccabees 2:61*

Hail Mary...

Trust God and he will help you; make straight your ways and hope in him. *Sirach 2:6*

Hail Mary...

Do not the tears that stream down her cheek cry out against him that causes them to fall? *Sirach 35:15*

Hail Mary...

He who serves God willingly is heard; his petition reaches the heavens. *Sirach 35:16*

Hail Mary...

Let us condemn him to a shameful death; for according to his own words, God will take care of him. *Wisdom 2:20*

Hail Mary...

Most admirable and worthy of everlasting remembrance was the mother who saw her seven sons perish in a single day, yet bore it courageously because of her hope in the LORD. *2 Maccabees 7:20*

Hail Mary...

Glory Be to the Father...

O My Jesus...

Fifth Sorrowful Mystery
Crucifixion

Your right hand, O LORD, magnificent in power, your
right hand, O LORD, has shattered the enemy.
Exodus 15:6

Our Father...

Then God said: "Take your son Isaac, your only one,
whom you love ... offer him up as a holocaust on a
height that I will point out to you." *Genesis 22:1*

Hail Mary...

Abel, for his part, brought one of the best firstlings of his
flock. The LORD looked with favor on Abel and his
offering. *Genesis 4:4*

Hail Mary...

The lamb must be a year-old male and without blemish
... it shall be slaughtered during the evening twilight.
Exodus 12:5-6

Hail Mary...

"Thus shall Aaron offer up the bullock, his sin offering,
to atone for himself and for his family. When he has
slaughtered it, he shall take a censer full of glowing
embers from the altar before the LORD..."
Leviticus 16:11-12

Hail Mary...

You shall not break any of its bones. The whole
community of Israel must keep this feast.
Exodus 12:46-47; [Numbers 9:12]

Hail Mary...

Will you not leave your riches to others, and your
earnings to be divided by lot?" *Sirach 14:15*

Hail Mary...

And you gave your sons good ground for hope that you
would permit repentance for their sins. *Wisdom 12:19*

Hail Mary...

How great the mercy of the LORD, his forgiveness of
those who return to him! *Sirach 17:24*

Hail Mary...

Next he tied up his son Isaac, and put him on top of the
wood on the altar. Then he reached out and took the
knife to slaughter his son. *Genesis 22:9-10*

Hail Mary...

"I know now how devoted you are to God, since you did
not withhold from me your own beloved son."
Genesis 22:12

Hail Mary...

Glory Be to the Father...

O My Jesus...

Hail Holy Queen...

The Glorious Mysteries

The Sign of the Cross

The Apostle's Creed

Sing to the LORD, for he is gloriously triumphant...
Exodus 15:21

Our Father...

For I know and believe that whatever God has spoken
will be accomplished. It shall happen, and not a single
word of the prophesies shall prove false. *Tobit 14:4*

Hail Mary for Faith

You who fear the LORD, hope for good things, for
lasting joy and mercy. *Sirach 2:9*

Hail Mary for Hope

Those who serve her serve the Holy One; those who love
her the LORD loves. *Sirach 4:14*

Hail Mary for Charity

Glory Be to the Father...

O My Jesus...

First Glorious Mystery
Resurrection

Be ready for the third day; for on the third day the
LORD will come down on Mount Sinai before the eyes of
all the people ... On the morning of the third day there
were peals of thunder and lightning, and a heavy cloud
over the mountain, and a very loud trumpet blast...
Exodus 19:11,16

Our Father...

All the fountains of the great abyss burst forth, and the
floodgates of the sky were opened. *Genesis 7:11*

Hail Mary...

She went down with him into the dungeon, and did not
desert him in his bonds, Until she brought him the
scepter of royalty and authority over his oppressors.
Wisdom 10:14

Hail Mary...

The days of eternity: who can number these? Heaven's
height, earth's breadth, the depths of the abyss: who can
explore these? *Sirach 1:2-3*

Hail Mary...

For love of your fathers he chose their descendants and
personally led you out of Egypt by his great power.
Deuteronomy 4:37

Hail Mary...

Limited are the days of one man's life, but the life of
Israel is days without number. *Sirach 37:23*

Hail Mary...

If you do good, know for whom you are doing it, and your kindness will have its effect. *Sirach 12:1*

Hail Mary...

In life he performed wonders, and after death, marvelous deeds. *Sirach 48:14*

Hail Mary...

Among brethren their leader is in honor; he who fears God is in honor among his people. *Sirach 10:20*

Hail Mary...

For I will sing the LORD's renown. Oh, proclaim the greatness of our God! *Deuteronomy 32:3*

Hail Mary...

I, the LORD, am your God. *Exodus 20:2*

Hail Mary...

Glory Be to the Father...

O My Jesus...

Second Glorious Mystery
Ascension

The LORD shall reign forever and ever. *Exodus 15:18*

Our Father...

Jerusalem, take off your robe of mourning and misery;
put on the splendor of glory from God forever...
Baruch 5:1

Hail Mary...

And now, O Lord, to you I turn my face and raise my
eyes. Bid me to depart from the earth... *Tobit 3:12-13*

Hail Mary...

All that is of earth returns to earth, and what is from
above returns above. *Sirach 40:11*

Hail Mary...

Whenever the ark set out, Moses would say, "Arise, O
LORD, that your enemies may be scattered, and those
who hate you may flee before you." *Numbers 10:35*

Hail Mary...

And when it came to rest, he would say, "Return, O
LORD, you who ride upon the clouds, to the troops of
Israel." *Numbers 10:36*

Hail Mary...

"Through those who approach me I will manifest my sacredness; In the sight of all the people I will reveal my glory." *Leviticus 10:3*

Hail Mary...

Who is like to you among the gods, O LORD? Who is like to you, magnificent in holiness? *Exodus 15:11*

Hail Mary...

The LORD will open up for you his rich treasure house of the heavens. *Deuteronomy 28:12*

Hail Mary...

In the highest heavens did I dwell, my throne on a pillar of cloud. The vault of heaven I compassed alone, through the deep abyss I wandered. *Sirach 24:4-5*

Hail Mary...

The heavens, even the highest heavens, belong to the LORD, your God, as well as the earth and everything on it. *Deuteronomy 10:14*

Hail Mary...

Glory Be to the Father...

O My Jesus...

Third Glorious Mystery
Descent of the Holy Spirit

To the Israelites the glory of the LORD was seen as a consuming fire on the mountaintop. *Exodus 24:17*

Our Father...

It was always so: during the day the Dwelling was covered by the cloud, which at night had the appearance of fire. *Numbers 9:16*

Hail Mary...

Out of the heavens he let you hear his voice to discipline you; on earth he let you see his great fire, and you heard him speaking out of the fire. *Deuteronomy 4:36*

Hail Mary...

Fix in your heart, that the LORD is God in the heavens above and on earth below, and that there is no other. *Deuteronomy 4:39*

Hail Mary...

The LORD, our God, has indeed let us see his glory and his majesty! We have heard his voice from the midst of the fire. *Deuteronomy 5:24*

Hail Mary...

For the LORD, your God, is a consuming fire, a jealous God. *Deuteronomy 4:24*

Hail Mary...

Ever present in your midst, I will be your God, and you will be my people; for it is I, the LORD, your God, who brought you out of the land of the Egyptians...
Leviticus 26:12-13

Hail Mary...

The gates of Jerusalem shall sing hymns of gladness, and all her house shall cry out, "Alleluia!" *Tobit 13:18*

Hail Mary...

For the spirit of the LORD fills the world, is all embracing, and knows what man says. *Wisdom 1:7*

Hail Mary...

Let your spirits rejoice in the mercy of God, and be not ashamed to give him praise. *Sirach 51:29*

Hail Mary...

Woe to you who have lost hope! What will you do at the visitation of the Lord? *Sirach 2:14*

Hail Mary...

Glory Be to the Father...

O My Jesus...

Fourth Glorious Mystery
Assumption

In your mercy you led the people you redeemed; in your strength you guided them to your holy dwelling.
Exodus 15:13

Our Father...

In whatever you do, remember your last days, and you will never sin. *Sirach 7:36*

Hail Mary...

Turn, O Jacob, and receive her: walk by her light toward splendor ... Blessed are we, O Israel; for what pleases God is known to us! *Baruch 4:2,4*

Hail Mary...

Blessed are you, daughter, by the Most High God, above all the women on earth... *Judith 13:18*

Hail Mary...

The LORD bless you and keep you. The LORD let his face shine upon you, and be gracious to you!
Numbers 6:24-25

Hail Mary...

"Blessed be God who has raised you up! May he be blessed for all ages!" For in you they shall praise his holy name forever. *Tobit 13:18*

Hail Mary...

A new hymn I will sing to my God. O LORD, great are you and glorious, wonderful in power and unsurpassable. *Judith 16:13*

Hail Mary...

The prayer of the lowly pierces the clouds; it does not rest till it reaches its goal... *Sirach 35:17*

Hail Mary...

For great is the power of God; by the humble he is glorified. *Sirach 3:19*

Hail Mary...

For those who keep the holy precepts hallowed shall he be found holy... *Wisdom 6:10*

Hail Mary...

To observe her laws is the basis for incorruptibility; and incorruptibility makes one close to God... *Wisdom 6:18-19*

Hail Mary...

Glory Be to the Father...

O My Jesus...

Fifth Glorious Mystery
Coronation

I will sing to the LORD, for he is gloriously triumphant.
Exodus 15:1

Our Father...

You have done good in Israel, and God is pleased with what you have wrought. May you be blessed by the LORD Almighty forever and ever! *Judith 15:10*

Hail Mary...

The God of your father, who helps you, God Almighty, who blesses you, With the blessings of the heavens above... *Genesis 49:25*

Hail Mary...

"He will then raise you high in praise and renown and glory above all other nations he has made, and you will be a people sacred to the LORD, your God, as he promised." *Deuteronomy 26:19*

Hail Mary...

Fear of the LORD is glory and splendor, gladness and a festive crown. *Sirach 1:9*

Hail Mary...

There is but one, wise and truly awe-inspiring, seated upon his throne: It is the LORD; he created her, has seen her and taken note of her. *Sirach 1:6-7*

Hail Mary...

Bless the LORD who has crowned you with glory!
Sirach 45:26

Hail Mary...

Therefore shall they receive the splendid crown, the
beauteous diadem, from the hand of the LORD...
Wisdom 5:16

Hail Mary...

Resplendent and unfading is Wisdom, and she is readily
perceived by those who love her, and found by those
who seek her. *Wisdom 6:12*

Hail Mary...

I give you thanks, O God of my father; I praise you, O
God my Savior! *Sirach 51:1*

Hail Mary...

Those who serve her serve the Holy One; those who love
her the LORD loves. *Sirach 4:14*

Hail Mary...

Glory Be to the Father...

O My Jesus...

Hail Holy Queen...

Gabriel, the Holy Spirit's Messenger

Daniel 6:22, 9:21; Luke 1:26; John 1:29

BOOK TWO
Old Testament Writings

"Truly your God is the God of gods and Lord of kings and a revealer of mysteries; that is why you were able to reveal this mystery." *Daniel 2:47*

The Our Father Meditation Verses

Selections from Daniel

The Hail Mary Meditation Verses

Selections from 1 Chronicles, 2 Chronicles, Daniel, Ecclesiastes, Esther, Ezra, Job, Lamentations, Nehemiah, Proverbs, Psalms, Ruth, and Song of Songs

The Joyful Mysteries

The Sign of the Cross

The Apostle's Creed

We follow you with our whole heart ... A joyful heart is the health of the body... *Daniel 3:41, Proverbs 17:22*

Our Father...

You have pronounced your decrees in justice and in perfect faithfulness. *Psalms 119:138*

Hail Mary for Faith

With awe-inspiring deeds of justice you answer us, O God our savior, The hope of all the ends of the earth and of the distant seas. *Psalms 65:6*

Hail Mary for Hope

I love the Lord. *Psalms 116:1*

Hail Mary for Charity

Glory Be to the Father...

O My Jesus...

First Joyful Mystery
Annunciation

"I was still occupied with this prayer, when Gabriel, the one whom I had seen before in vision, came to me in rapid flight at the time of the evening sacrifice."
Daniel 9:21

Our Father...

You are all-beautiful, my beloved, and there is no blemish in you. *Song of Songs 4:7*

Hail Mary...

He instructed me in these words: "Daniel, I have now come to give you understanding. When you began your petition, an answer was given which I have come to announce, because you are beloved." *Daniel 9:22-23*

Hail Mary...

If you receive my words ... then will you understand the fear of the LORD; the knowledge of God you will find... *Proverbs 2:1,5*

Hail Mary...

Happy is he who trusts in the LORD! The wise man is esteemed for his discernment... *Proverbs 16:20-21*

Hail Mary...

Entrust your works to the LORD... trust in the LORD with all your heart. *Proverbs 16:3; 3:5*

Hail Mary...

Those who love me I also love, and those who seek me find me. *Proverbs 8:17*

Hail Mary...

He gives wisdom to the wise and knowledge to those who understand. *Daniel 2:21*

Hail Mary...

Angels of the Lord, bless the Lord, praise and exalt him above all forever. *Daniel 3:58*

Hail Mary...

Did not he who made me in the womb make him? Did not the same One fashion us before our birth? *Job 31:15*

Hail Mary...

O, most beautiful among women. *Song of Songs 1:8*

Hail Mary...

Glory Be to the Father...

O My Jesus...

Second Joyful Mystery
Visitation

He reveals deep and hidden things and knows what is in the darkness, for the light dwells with him. *Daniel 2:22*

Our Father...

In all your ways be mindful of him, and he will make straight your paths. *Proverbs 3:6*

Hail Mary...

Take your places, stand firm, and see how the LORD will be with you to deliver you, Judah and Jerusalem. Do not fear or lose heart. Tomorrow go out to meet them, and the LORD will be with you. *2 Chronicles 20:17*

Hail Mary...

He who walks honestly walks securely... *Proverbs 10:9*

Hail Mary...

Walk in the way of good men, and keep to the paths of the just ... walk with wise men and you will become wise... *Proverbs 2:20; 13:20*

Hail Mary...

On the way of wisdom I direct you, I lead you on straightforward paths. *Proverbs 4:11*

Hail Mary...

You may securely go your way; your foot will never stumble. *Proverbs 3:23*

Hail Mary...

He is the shield of those who walk honestly, guarding the paths of justice, protecting the way of his pious ones. *Proverbs 2:7-8*

Hail Mary...

You will understand rectitude and justice, honesty, every good path; for wisdom will enter your heart, knowledge will please your soul. *Proverbs 2:9-10*

Hail Mary...

My inmost being will exult, when your lips speak what is right. *Proverbs 23:16*

Hail Mary...

She opens her mouth in wisdom, and on her tongue is kindly counsel. *Proverbs 31:26*

Hail Mary...

Glory Be to the Father...

O My Jesus...

Third Joyful Mystery
Nativity

He is a deliverer and savior, working signs and wonders in heaven and on earth... *Daniel 6:28*

Our Father...

When he established the heavens I was there ... the LORD has made everything for his own ends...
Proverbs 8:27; 16:4

Hail Mary...

Blessed is the LORD who has not failed to provide you today with an heir! May he become famous in Israel!... They called him Obed. He was the father of Jesse, the father of David. *Ruth 4:14,17*

Hail Mary...

The LORD begot me, the first born of his ways, the forerunner of his prodigies of long ago..." *Proverbs 8:22*

Hail Mary...

What, my son, my first-born! What, O son of my womb; What, O son of my vows! *Proverbs 31:2*

Hail Mary...

Yours is princely power in the day of your birth, in holy splendor; before the daystar, like the dew, I have begotten you ... Even in his royalty he was poor at birth. *Psalms 110:3; Ecclesiastes 4:14*

Hail Mary...

When you lie down she will watch over you, and when you wake, she will share your concerns; wherever you turn, she will guide you. *Proverbs 6:22*

Hail Mary...

She obtains wool and flax and makes cloth with skillful hands. *Proverbs 31:13*

Hail Mary...

What is this coming up from the desert, like a column of smoke laden with myrrh, with frankincense, and with the perfume of every exotic dust? *Song of Songs 3:6*

Hail Mary...

Bring gifts, and enter his presence; worship the LORD in holy attire. *1 Chronicles 16:29*

Hail Mary...

The kings of Tarshish and the Isles shall offer gifts; the kings of Arabia and Seba shall bring tribute. All kings shall pay homage, all nations shall serve him. *Psalms 72:10-11*

Hail Mary...

Glory Be to the Father...

O My Jesus...

Fourth Joyful Mystery
Presentation

"Ah, Lord, great and awesome God, you who keep your merciful covenant toward those who love you and observe your commandments!" *Daniel 9:4*

Our Father...

Guard your step when you go to the house of God. Let your approach be obedience... *Ecclesiastes 4:17*

Hail Mary...

We have agreed to bring each year to the house of the LORD the first fruits of our fields ... the first-born of our children... *Nehemiah 10:36-37*

Hail Mary...

Honor the LORD with your wealth, with the first fruits of all your produce... *Proverbs 3:9*

Hail Mary...

O My God! Let not the devotion which I showed for the house of my God and its services be forgotten!
Nehemiah 13:14

Hail Mary...

Priests of the Lord, bless the Lord; praise and exalt him above all forever. *Daniel 3:84*

Hail Mary...

I have dealt with great things that I do not understand; things too wonderful for me, which I cannot know. *Job 42:3-4*

Hail Mary...

I had heard of you by word of mouth, but now my eye has seen you. *Job 42:5*

Hail Mary...

On the first day of the fifth month he arrived at Jerusalem, for the favoring hand of his God was upon him. Ezra had set his heart on the study and practice of the law of the LORD and on teaching statutes and ordinances in Israel. *Ezra 7:9-10*

Hail Mary...

Fear God and keep his commandments, for this is man's all; because God will bring to judgment every work, with all its hidden qualities... *Ecclesiastes 12:13*

Hail Mary...

This is the day the LORD has made; let us be glad and rejoice in it. *Psalms 118:24*

Hail Mary...

Glory Be to the Father...

O My Jesus...

Fifth Joyful Mystery
Finding in the Temple

Blessed are you in the temple of your holy glory,
praiseworthy and glorious above all forever.
Daniel 3:53

Our Father...

Remember your Creator in the days of your youth,
before the evil days come and the years approach of
which you will say, I have no pleasure in them.
Ecclesiastes 12:1

Hail Mary...

My son, forget not my teaching, keep in mind my
commands; for many days, and years of life, and peace,
will they bring you. *Proverbs 3:1-2*

Hail Mary...

It is he who shall build a house in my honor; he shall be
a son to me, and I will be a father to him, and I will
establish the throne of his kingship over Israel forever.
1 Chronicles 22:10

Hail Mary...

Now, my son, the LORD be with you, and may you
succeed in building the house of the LORD your God, as
he has said you shall. *1 Chronicles 22:11*

Hail Mary...

I will open my mouth in a parable, I will utter mysteries
from of old. *Psalms 78:2*

Hail Mary...

Sincere are all the words of my mouth ... receive my instruction in preference to silver, and knowledge rather than choice gold. *Proverbs 8:8,10*

Hail Mary...

By wisdom is a house built, by understanding is it made firm... *Proverbs 24:3*

Hail Mary...

Who is like the wise man, and who knows the explanation of things? A man's wisdom illumines his face... *Ecclesiastes 8:1*

Hail Mary...

You worked signs and wonders against Pharaoh, against all his servants and the people of his land, because you knew of their insolence toward them; thus you made for yourself a name even to this day. *Nehemiah 9:10*

Hail Mary...

"You are a priest forever, according to the order of Melchizedek." *Psalms 110:4*

Hail Mary...

Glory Be to the Father...

O My Jesus...

Hail Holy Queen...

The Sorrowful Mysteries

The Sign of the Cross

The Apostle's Creed

So let our sacrifice be in your presence today as we
follow you unreservedly; for those who trust in you
cannot be put to shame. *Daniel 3:40*

Our Father...

No one who waits for you shall be put to shame; those
shall be put to shame who heedlessly break faith.
Psalms 25:3

Hail Mary for Faith

Yet even now there remains a hope for Israel. *Ezra 10:2*

Hail Mary for Hope

"You have remembered me, O God," said Daniel; "you
have not forsaken those who love you." *Daniel 14:38*

Hail Mary for Charity

Glory Be to the Father...

O My Jesus...

First Sorrowful Mystery
Agony in the Garden

Do not let us be put to shame, but deal with us in your kindness and great mercy. Deliver us by your wonders, and bring glory to your name, O Lord. *Daniel 3:42-43*

Our Father...

My groans are many, and I am sick at heart.
Lamentations 1:22

Hail Mary...

Rescue those who are being dragged to death, and from those tottering to execution withdraw not.
Proverbs 24:11

Hail Mary...

At this I weep, my eyes run with tears: Far from me are all who could console me, any who might revive me.
Lamentations 1:16

Hail Mary...

I have no peace nor ease; I have no rest, for trouble comes! *Job 3:26*

Hail Mary...

What strength have I that I should endure, and what is my limit that I should be patient? *Job 6:11*

Hail Mary...

The breakers of death surged round about me ... the
cords of the nether world enmeshed me ... in my distress
I called upon the LORD and cried out to my God ... my
cry to him reached his ears. *Psalms 18:5-7*

Hail Mary...

You came to my aid when I called to you; you said,
"Have no fear!" *Lamentations 3:57*

Hail Mary...

I am exhausted and stunned, all my company has closed
in on me. As a witness there rises up my traducer,
speaking openly against me... *Job 16:7-8*

Hail Mary...

Deceit is in the hands of those who plot evil ... some
friends bring ruin on us. *Proverbs 12:20; 18:24*

Hail Mary...

Do not those who plot evil go astray? The false witness
will not go unpunished, and he who utters lies will
perish. *Proverbs 14:22; 19:9*

Hail Mary...

Glory Be to the Father...

O My Jesus...

Second Sorrowful Mystery
Scourging

Blessed is the man who has patience and perseveres until the one thousand three hundred and thirty five days. Go, take your rest, you shall rise for your reward at the end of days. *Daniel 12:12-13*

Our Father...

How long will you set upon a man and all together beat him down as though he were a sagging fence, a battered wall? *Psalms 62:4*

Hail Mary...

A degrading beating will he get, and his disgrace will not be wiped away... *Proverbs 6:33*

Hail Mary...

The prating of some men is like sword thrusts... *Proverbs 12:18*

Hail Mary...

You hear their insults, O LORD ... the whispered murmurings of my foes, against me all the day. *Lamentations 3:61-62*

Hail Mary...

He left me desolate, in pain all the day. *Lamentations 1:13*

Hail Mary...

The patient man shows much good sense ... he who spares his words is truly wise... *Proverbs 14:29; 17:27*

Hail Mary...

Evil is cleansed away by bloody lashes, and a scourging to the inmost being. *Proverbs 20:30*

Hail Mary...

All speech is labored; there is nothing man can say. The eye is not satisfied with seeing nor is the ear filled with hearing. *Ecclesiastes 1:8*

Hail Mary...

There is an appointed time for everything ... a time to be silent, and a time to speak. *Ecclesiastes 3:1,7*

Hail Mary...

Were one to offer all he owns to purchase love, he would be roundly mocked. *Song of Songs 8:7*

Hail Mary...

Glory Be to the Father...

O My Jesus...

Third Sorrowful Mystery
Crowning with Thorns

His dominion is an everlasting dominion that shall not be taken away, his kingship shall not be destroyed. *Daniel 7:14*

>*Our Father...*

The stirring of anger brings forth blood. *Proverbs 30:33*

>*Hail Mary...*

Men will curse him, people will denounce him. *Proverbs 24:24*

>*Hail Mary...*

The anointed one of the LORD, our breath of life, was caught in their snares. *Lamentations 4:20*

>*Hail Mary...*

He has veiled my path in darkness; he has stripped me of my glory, and taken the diadem from my brow. He breaks me down on every side... *Job 19:8-10*

>*Hail Mary...*

"I have all but come to utter ruin, condemned by the public assembly!" *Proverbs 5:14*

>*Hail Mary...*

Zion stretched out her hands, but there was no one to console her ... all my enemies rejoice at my misfortune... *Lamentations 1:17,21*

>*Hail Mary...*

So long as I still have life in me and the breath of God is in my nostrils, my lips shall not speak falsehood ... I will not renounce my innocence. *Job 27:3-5*

Hail Mary...

Better is the end of speech than its beginning; better is the patient spirit than the lofty spirit. *Ecclesiastes 7:8*

Hail Mary...

I am a worm, not a man; the scorn of men, despised by the people. All who see me scoff at me; they mock me with parted lips, they wag their heads... *Psalms 22:7-8*

Hail Mary...

Behold, I have prepared my case, I know that I am in the right. If anyone can make a case against me, then I shall be silent and die. *Job 13:18-19*

Hail Mary...

Glory Be to the Father...

O My Jesus...

Fourth Sorrowful Mystery
Carrying of the Cross

For you are just in all you have done; all your deeds are faultless, all your ways right, and all your judgments proper. *Daniel 3:27*

Our Father...

He has counsel in store for the upright, he is the shield of those who walk honestly... *Proverbs 2:7*

Hail Mary...

In his mind a man plans his course, but the LORD directs his steps. *Proverbs 16:9*

Hail Mary...

On the way of duty I walk, along the paths of justice ... the LORD is a stronghold to him who walks honestly. *Proverbs 8:20; 10:29*

Hail Mary...

Come, all you who pass by the way, look and see whether there is any suffering like my suffering... *Lamentations 1:12*

Hail Mary...

My foot has always walked in his steps; his way I have kept and have not turned aside. *Job 23:11*

Hail Mary...

He who oppresses the poor blasphemes his Maker, but
he who is kind to the needy glorifies him.
Proverbs 14:31

Hail Mary...

They have settled about my neck, he has brought my
strength to its knees; the Lord has delivered me into
their grip, I am unable to rise. *Lamentations 1:14*

Hail Mary...

You groan in the end, when your flesh and your body
are consumed. *Proverbs 5:11*

Hail Mary...

Has God forgotten pity? A man's spirit sustains him in
infirmity... *Psalms 77:10; Proverbs 18:14*

Hail Mary...

Sorrow is better than laughter, because when the face is
sad the heart grows wiser. *Ecclesiastes 7:3*

Hail Mary...

Glory Be to the Father...

O My Jesus...

Fifth Sorrowful Mystery
Crucifixion

"O eternal God, you know what is hidden and are aware of all things before they come to be: you know that they have testified falsely against me. Here I am about to die, though I have done none of the things with which these wicked men have charged me." *Daniel 13:42-43*

Our Father...

What profit has man from all the labor which he toils at under the sun? In all labor there is profit.
Ecclesiastes 1:3; Proverbs 14:23

Hail Mary...

Be not afraid of sudden terror, of the ruin of the wicked when it comes; for the LORD will be your confidence.
Proverbs 3:25-26

Hail Mary...

He pierces my sides with shafts from his quiver ... the thought of my homeless poverty is wormwood and gall.
Lamentations 3:13,19

Hail Mary...

Cry out to the Lord; moan, O daughter Zion! Let your tears flow like a torrent day and night.
Lamentations 2:18

Hail Mary...

As he came forth from his mother's womb, so again shall he depart, naked as he came, having nothing from his labor that he can carry in his hand. *Ecclesiastes 5:14*

Hail Mary...

They meet with darkness in the daytime, and at noonday they grope as though it were night. *Job 5:14*

Hail Mary...

He pierces my sides without mercy, he pours out my gall upon the ground. He pierces me with thrust upon thrust... *Job 16:13-14*

Hail Mary...

My God, my God, why have you forsaken me?
Psalms 22:1

Hail Mary...

Your hands have formed me and fashioned me; will you then turn and destroy me? Why then did you bring me forth from the womb? *Job 10:8,18*

Hail Mary...

The LORD saved his people and delivered us from all these evils. God worked signs and great wonders, such as have not occurred among the nations. *Esther 10:6*

Hail Mary...

Glory Be to the Father...

O My Jesus...

Hail Holy Queen...

The Glorious Mysteries

The Sign of the Cross

The Apostle's Creed

Deliver us by your wonders, and bring glory to your name: O Lord. *Daniel 3:43*

Our Father...

My eyes are upon the faithful of the land, that they may dwell with me. *Psalms 101:6*

Hail Mary for Faith

For what do I wait, O Lord? In you is my hope. *Psalms 39:8*

Hail Mary for Hope

There is an appointed time for everything ... a time to love ... a time of peace. *Ecclesiastes 3:1,8*

Hail Mary for Charity

Glory Be to the Father...

O My Jesus...

First Glorious Mystery
Resurrection

For he has delivered us from the nether world, and saved us from the power of death; He has freed us from the raging flame and delivered us from the fire.
Daniel 3:88

Our Father...

The nether world and the abyss lie open before the LORD... *Proverbs 15:11*

Hail Mary...

The favors of the LORD are not exhausted, his mercies are not spent; They are renewed each morning so great is his faithfulness. *Lamentations 3:22-23*

Hail Mary...

Whatever God does will endure forever; there is no adding to it, or taking from it. Thus has God done that he may be revered. *Ecclesiastes 3:14*

Hail Mary...

Just as you know not how the breath of life fashions the human frame in the mother's womb, So you know not the work of God which he is accomplishing in the universe. *Ecclesiastes 11:5*

Hail Mary...

If a king is zealous for the rights of the poor, his throne stands firm forever. *Proverbs 29:14*

Hail Mary...

You, O LORD, are enthroned forever; your throne stands from age to age. *Lamentations 5:19*

Hail Mary...

He who finds me finds life, and wins favor from the LORD. *Proverbs 8:35*
Hail Mary...

For he is the living God, enduring forever; his kingdom shall not be destroyed, and his dominion shall be without end. *Daniel 6:27*

Hail Mary...

"Blessed is your glorious name, and exalted above all blessing and praise." *Nehemiah 9:5*

Hail Mary...

The heavens proclaim his justice, and all the peoples see his glory. *Psalms 97:6*

Hail Mary...

Glory Be to the Father...

O My Jesus...

Second Glorious Mystery
Ascension

One like a son of man coming, on the clouds of heaven;
When he reached the Ancient One and was presented
before him, He received dominion, glory, and kingship...
Daniel 7:13-14

Our Father...

"It is you, O LORD, you are the only one; you made the
heavens, the highest heavens and all their host, the earth
and all that is upon it, the seas and all that is in them."
Nehemiah 9:6

Hail Mary...

Let them know that you alone are the Lord God, glorious
over the whole world. *Daniel 3:45*

Hail Mary...

Therefore, I, Nebuchadnezzar, now praise and exalt and
glorify the King of heaven, because all his works are
right and his ways just; and those who walk in pride he
is able to humble. *Daniel 4:34*

Hail Mary...

Splendor and majesty go before him; praise and joy are
in his holy place.   *1 Chronicles 16:27*

Hail Mary...

Give to the LORD, you families of nations, give to the
LORD glory and praise; give to the LORD the glory due
his name! *1 Chronicles 16:28*

Hail Mary...

"Yours, O LORD, are grandeur and power, majesty, splendor, and glory. For all in heaven and on earth is yours; yours, O LORD is the sovereignty; you are exalted as head over all. *1 Chronicles 29:11*

Hail Mary...

Thrones were set up and the Ancient One took his throne. His clothing was snow bright, and the hair on his head as white as wool; His throne was flames of fire, with wheels of burning fire. *Daniel 7:9*

Hail Mary...

Blessed are you on the throne of your kingdom, praiseworthy and exalted above all forever.
Daniel 3:54

Hail Mary...

Blessed are you, and praiseworthy, O Lord, the God of our fathers, and glorious forever is your name.
Daniel 3:26

Hail Mary...

You are clothed with majesty and glory, robed in light ... you make the clouds your chariot; you travel on the wings of the wind. *Psalms 104:1,3*

Hail Mary...

Glory Be to the Father...

O My Jesus...

Third Glorious Mystery
Descent of the Holy Spirit

Holy men of humble heart, bless the Lord; praise and exalt him above all forever. *Daniel 3:87*

Our Father...

The hope of the just brings them joy... *Proverbs 10:28*

Hail Mary...

Every word of God is tested; he is a shield to those who take refuge in him. *Proverbs 30:5*

Hail Mary...

Lo! I will pour out to you my spirit, I will acquaint you with my words. *Proverbs 1:23*

Hail Mary...

The fear of the LORD is the beginning of knowledge...
Proverbs 1:7

Hail Mary...

Good is the LORD to one who waits for him, to the soul that seeks him; It is good to hope in silence for the saving help of the LORD. *Lamentations 3:25-26*

Hail Mary...

Trust in the LORD and he will help you. *Proverbs 20:22*

Hail Mary...

"Your good spirit you bestowed on them, to give them understanding; your manna you did not withhold from their mouths, and you gave them water in their thirst."
Nehemiah 9:20

Hail Mary...

The Lord by wisdom founded the earth, established the heavens by understanding; By his knowledge the depths break open, and the clouds drop down dew.
Proverbs 3:19-20

Hail Mary...

Sing to the LORD, all the earth, announce his salvation, day after day. Tell his glory among the nations; among all peoples, his wondrous deeds. *1 Chronicles 16:23-24*

Hail Mary...

O LORD, my God, you are great indeed! You make the winds your messengers, and flaming fire your ministers.
Psalms 104:1,4

Hail Mary...

Glory Be to the Father...

O My Jesus...

Fourth Glorious Mystery
Assumption

Know that the Most High rules over the kingdom of
men: He can give it to whom he will or set over it the
lowliest of men. *Daniel 4:14*

Our Father...

To what can I liken or compare you, O daughter
Jerusalem ... virgin daughter Zion? Many are the
women of proven worth, but you have excelled them all.
Lamentations 2:13; Proverbs 31:29

Hail Mary...

"Arise, bless the LORD, your God, from eternity to
eternity!" *Nehemiah 9:5*

Hail Mary...

Let us reach out our hearts toward God in heaven!
Lamentations 3:41
Hail Mary...

"Arise, my beloved, my beautiful one, and come!"
Song of Songs 2:10
Hail Mary...

Who is this that comes forth like the dawn, as beautiful
as the moon, as resplendent as the sun?
Song of Songs 6:10
Hail Mary...

He who is humble of spirit obtains honor ... you win
favor and good esteem before God and man.
Proverbs 29:23; 3:4
Hail Mary...

The LORD loves the pure of heart... *Proverbs 22:11*

Hail Mary...

As a lily among thorns, so is my beloved among women.
Song of Songs 2:2

Hail Mary...

He sets up on high the lowly, and those who mourn he
exalts to safety. *Job 5:11*

Hail Mary...

Not to us, O LORD, not to us but to your name give
glory because of your kindness, because of your truth.
Psalms 115:1

Hail Mary...

Glory Be to the Father...

O My Jesus...

Fifth Glorious Mystery
Coronation

How great are his signs, how mighty his wonders; his kingdom an everlasting kingdom, and his dominion endures through all generations. *Daniel 3:100*

Our Father...

For great is the LORD and highly to be praised; and awesome is he, beyond all gods. *1 Chronicles 16:25*

Hail Mary...

For all the gods of the nations are things of nought, but the LORD made the heavens. *1 Chronicles 16:26*

Hail Mary...

God will bring to judgment every work, with all its hidden qualities, whether good or bad.
Ecclesiastes 12:13

Hail Mary...

He who sows virtue has a sure reward. *Proverbs 11:18*

Hail Mary...

The woman who fears the LORD is to be praised. Give her a reward of her labors, and let her works praise her at the city gates. *Proverbs 31:30-31*

Hail Mary...

The good man wins favor from the LORD... *Proverbs 12:2*

Hail Mary...

The reward of humility and fear of the LORD is riches, honor and life. *Proverbs 22:4*

Hail Mary...

Daughters of Jerusalem, come forth and look upon King Solomon In the crown with which his mother has crowned him ... on the day of the joy of his heart. *Song of Songs 3:11*

Hail Mary...

A graceful diadem will they be for your head ... she is clothed with strength and dignity... *Proverbs 1:9; 31:25*

Hail Mary...

You are all-beautiful, my beloved, and there is no blemish in you. *Song of Songs 4:7*

Hail Mary...

Glory Be to the Father...

O My Jesus...

Hail Holy Queen...

Three Days
Jonah 2:1-11; Matthew 12:40; Luke 11:30

BOOK THREE
Old Testament Prophets

From now on I announce new things to you, hidden events of which you knew not. *Isaiah 48:6*

The Our Father Meditation Verses

Selections from Isaiah

The Hail Mary Meditation Verses

Selections from Amos, Ezekiel, Habakkuk, Haggai, Hosea, Isaiah, Jeremiah, Joel, Jonah, Joshua, Judges, 1 Kings, 2 Kings, Malachi, Micah, Nahum, Obadiah, 1 Samuel, 2 Samuel, Zechariah, Zephaniah

The Joyful Mysteries

The Sign of the Cross

The Apostle's Creed

I rejoice heartily in the LORD, in my God is the joy of my soul... *Isaiah 61:10*

Our Father...

"Toward the faithful you are faithful; toward the wholehearted you are wholehearted; Toward the sincere you are sincere..." *2 Samuel 22:26-27*

Hail Mary for Faith

O Hope of Israel, O LORD, our Savior in time of need! *Jeremiah 14:8*

Hail Mary for Hope

He will rejoice over you with gladness, and renew you in his love... *Zephaniah 3:17*

Hail Mary for Charity

Glory Be to the Father...

O My Jesus...

First Joyful Mystery
Annunciation

Therefore the Lord himself will give you this sign: the virgin shall be with child, and bear a son, and shall name him Immanuel. *Isaiah 7:14*

Our Father...

Keep this book of the law on your lips. Recite it by day and by night, that you may observe carefully all that is written in it; then you will successfully attain your goal. *Joshua 1:8*

Hail Mary...

Gideon, now aware that it had been the angel of the LORD said "Alas, Lord God, that I have seen the angel of the LORD face to face!" *Judges 6:22*

Hail Mary...

The LORD answered him, "Be calm, do not fear. You shall not die." *Judges 6:23*

Hail Mary...

But now, thus says the LORD, who created you, O Jacob, and formed you, O Israel: Fear not, for I have redeemed you; I have called you by name: you are mine. *Isaiah 43:1*

Hail Mary...

The King of Israel, the LORD, is in your midst, you have no further misfortune to fear. *Zephaniah 3:15*

Hail Mary...

For I am with you ... and my spirit continues in your midst; do not fear! *Haggai 2:4-5*

Hail Mary...

God indeed is my savior; I am confident and unafraid. My strength and my courage is the LORD, and he has been my savior. *Isaiah 12:2*

Hail Mary...

Before I formed you in the womb I knew you, before you were born I dedicated you, a prophet to the nations I appointed you. *Jeremiah 1:5*

Hail Mary...

I will raise up your heir after you ... I will make his kingdom firm. *2 Samuel 7:12*

Hail Mary...

For now the LORD has spoken who formed me as his servant from the womb ... I am made glorious in the sight of the LORD, and my God is now my strength! *Isaiah 49:5*

Hail Mary...

Glory Be to the Father...

O My Jesus...

Second Joyful Mystery
Visitation

A voice cries out: In the desert prepare the way of the LORD! Make straight in the wasteland a highway for our God! *Isaiah 40:3*

Our Father...

I am the LORD, the God of all mankind! Is anything impossible to me? *Jeremiah 32:27*

Hail Mary...

"O LORD of hosts, if you look with pity on the misery of your handmaid, if you remember me and do not forget me, if you give your handmaid a male child, I will give him to the LORD as long as he lives." *1 Samuel 1:11*

Hail Mary...

Lo, I am sending my messenger to prepare the way before me ... Yes, he is coming, says the LORD of hosts. *Malachi 3:1*

Hail Mary...

You will be with child and will bear a son ... For the boy shall be consecrated to God from the womb ... The boy grew up and the LORD blessed him. *Judges 13:7,24*

Hail Mary...

Let him who is wise understand these things; let him who is prudent know them. Straight are the paths of the LORD, in them the just walk... *Hosea 14:10*

Hail Mary...

"Come, let us climb the mount of the LORD, to the house of the God of Jacob, That he may instruct us in his ways, that we may walk in his paths." *Micah 4:2*

Hail Mary...

Listen, O distant peoples. The LORD called me from birth, from my mother's womb he gave me my name. *Isaiah 49:1*

Hail Mary...

Render true judgment, and show kindness and compassion toward each other. *Zechariah 7:9*

Hail Mary...

"My heart exults in the LORD, my horn is exalted in my God." *1 Samuel 2:1*

Hail Mary...

You are my witnesses, says the LORD, my servants whom I have chosen To know and believe in me and understand that it is I. *Isaiah 43:10*

Hail Mary...

Glory Be to the Father...

O My Jesus...

Third Joyful Mystery
Nativity

For a child is born to us, a son is given us; upon his shoulder dominion rests. They name him Wonder-Counselor, God-Hero, Father-Forever, Prince of Peace. *Isaiah 9:5*

Our Father...

Blow the trumpet in Zion, sound the alarm on my holy mountain! Let all who dwell in the land tremble, for the day of the LORD is coming. *Joel 2:1*

Hail Mary...

The days are coming, says the LORD, when I will fulfill the promise I made to the house of Israel and Judah. *Jeremiah 33:14*

Hail Mary...

Therefore the Lord will give them up, until the time when she who is to give birth has borne... *Micah 5:2*

Hail Mary...

Rejoice heartily, O daughter Zion, shout for joy, O daughter Jerusalem! See, your king shall come to you; a just savior is he. *Zechariah 9:9*

Hail Mary...

See, I am coming to dwell among you, says the LORD. Many nations shall join themselves to the LORD on that day, and they shall be his people... *Zechariah 2:14-15*

Hail Mary...

Hear, O kings! Give ear, O princes! I to the LORD will sing my song, my hymn to the LORD, the God of Israel. *Judges 5:3*

Hail Mary...

An ox knows its owner, and an ass, its master's manger; But Israel does not know, my people has not understood. *Isaiah 1:3*

Hail Mary...

Shout with exultation, O city of Zion, for great in your midst is the Holy One of Israel! *Isaiah 12:6*

Hail Mary...

Do you not know? Have you not heard? Was it not foretold you from the beginning? *Isaiah 40:21*

Hail Mary...

Thus says the LORD, Israel's King and redeemer, the LORD of hosts: I am the first and I am the last; there is no God but me. *Isaiah 44:6*

Hail Mary...

Glory Be to the Father...

O My Jesus...

Fourth Joyful Mystery
Presentation

But a shoot shall sprout from the stump of Jesse, and from his roots a bud shall blossom. The spirit of the LORD shall rest upon him: a spirit of wisdom and of understanding. *Isaiah 11:1-2*

Our Father...

Be very careful to observe the precept and law which Moses, the servant of the LORD, enjoined upon you: love the LORD, your God; follow him faithfully; keep his commandments; remain loyal to him; and serve him with your whole heart and soul. *Joshua 22:5*

Hail Mary...

In those days, in that time, I will raise up for David a just shoot; he shall do what is right and just in the land. *Jeremiah 33:15*

Hail Mary...

Seek the LORD, all you humble of the earth, who have observed his law; Seek justice, seek humility. *Zephaniah 2:3*

Hail Mary...

You are my witnesses, says the LORD. I am God, yes, from eternity I am He ... See, I am doing something new! Now it springs forth, do you not perceive it? *Isaiah 43:12,19*

Hail Mary...

Remember the law of Moses my servant ... the statues and ordinances for all Israel. *Malachi 3:22*

Hail Mary...

Above all, be firm and steadfast, taking care to observe the entire law ... Do not swerve from it either to the right or to the left, that you may succeed wherever you go. *Joshua 1:7*

Hail Mary...

He shall stand firm and shepherd his flock by the strength of the LORD, in the majestic name of the LORD, his God ... he shall be peace. *Micah 5:3*

Hail Mary...

The LORD is in his holy temple; silence before him, all the earth! *Habakkuk 2:20*

Hail Mary...

See, I am laying a stone in Zion, a stone that has been tested, A precious cornerstone as a sure foundation; he who puts his faith in it shall not be shaken. *Isaiah 28:16*

Hail Mary...

When Israel was a child I loved him, out of Egypt I called my son. *Hosea 11:1*

Hail Mary...

Glory Be to the Father...

O My Jesus...

Fifth Joyful Mystery
Finding in the Temple

For from Zion shall go forth instruction, and the word of the LORD from Jerusalem. *Isaiah 2:3*

Our Father...

I will be a father to him, and he shall be a son to me. *2 Samuel 7:14*

Hail Mary...

The Lord will give you the bread you need and the water for which you thirst. No longer will your Teacher hide himself, but with your own eyes you shall see your Teacher. *Isaiah 30:20*

Hail Mary...

Rejoice in the LORD, your God! He has given you the teacher of justice. *Joel 2:23*

Hail Mary...

For from Zion shall go instruction, and the word of the LORD from Jerusalem. *Micah 4:2*

Hail Mary...

True doctrine was in his mouth, and no dishonesty was found upon his lips; He walked with me in integrity and uprightness, and turned many away from evil. *Malachi 2:6*

Hail Mary...

For thus says the Lord GOD: I myself will look after and tend my sheep. As a shepherd tends his flock when he finds himself among his scattered sheep, so will I tend my sheep. *Ezekiel 34:11-12*

Hail Mary...

"The temple of the LORD!" Only if you thoroughly reform your ways and your deeds ... will I remain with you in this place, in the land which I gave your fathers long ago and forever. *Jeremiah 7:4-5, 7*

Hail Mary...

Them I will bring to my holy mountain and make joyful in my house of prayer... *Isaiah 56:7*

Hail Mary...

It is he who shall build a house for my name. And I will make his royal throne firm forever. *2 Samuel 7:13*

Hail Mary...

"Now indeed I know that you are a man of God," the woman replied to Elijah. "The word of the LORD comes truly from your mouth." *1 Kings 17:24*

Hail Mary...

Glory Be to the Father...

O My Jesus...

Hail Holy Queen...

The Sorrowful Mysteries

The Sign of the Cross

The Apostle's Creed

Why did I come forth from the womb, to see sorrow and pain, to end my days in shame? *Jeremiah 20:18*

Our Father...

We will truly and faithfully follow all the instructions the LORD, your God, will send us. Whether it is pleasant or difficult, we will obey the command of the LORD our God... *Jeremiah 42:5*

Hail Mary for Faith

You never said, "It is hopeless"; New strength you found, and so you did not weaken. Of whom were you afraid? *Isaiah 57:10-11*

Hail Mary for Hope

You have been told, O man, what is good, and what the LORD requires of you: Only to do the right and love goodness and to walk humbly with your God. *Micah 6:8*

Hail Mary for Charity

Glory Be to the Father...

O My Jesus...

First Sorrowful Mystery
Agony in the Garden

But the LORD laid upon him the guilt of us all.
Isaiah 53:6

Our Father...

Your misfortunes are double; who is there to console
with you? Desolation and destruction, famine and
sword! Who is there to comfort you? *Isaiah 51:19*

Hail Mary...

"O LORD, my rock, my fortress, my deliverer, my God,
my rock of refuge!" *2 Samuel 22:2*

Hail Mary...

O LORD, you have marked him for judgment, O Rock,
you have readied him for punishment! *Habakkuk 1:12*

Hail Mary...

Why do you let me see ruin: why must I look at misery?
Destruction and violence are before me... *Habakkuk 1:3*

Hail Mary...

But you brought up my life from the pit, O LORD, my
God. When my soul fainted within me, I remembered
the LORD; My prayer reached you in your holy temple.
Jonah 2:7-8

Hail Mary...

How long, O LORD? I cry for help but you do not listen!
Habakkuk 1:2

Hail Mary...

But I, with resounding praise, will sacrifice to you; What
I have vowed I will pay: deliverance is from the LORD.
Jonah 2:10

Hail Mary...

Out of my distress I called to the LORD, and he
answered me; From the midst of the nether world I cried
for help, and you heard my voice. *Jonah 2:3*

Hail Mary...

They will fight against you, but not prevail over you, for
I am with you to deliver you. *Jeremiah 1:19*

Hail Mary...

The LORD is good, a refuge on the day of distress; He
takes care of those who have recourse to him, when the
flood rages. *Nahum 1:7-8*

Hail Mary...

Glory Be to the Father...

O My Jesus...

Second Sorrowful Mystery
Scourging

I gave my back to those who beat me, my cheeks to those who plucked my beard; My face I did not shield from buffets and spitting. *Isaiah 50:6*

Our Father...

The breakers of death surged round about me, the floods of perdition overwhelmed me. *2 Samuel 22:5*

Hail Mary...

I will put it into the hands of your tormentors, those who ordered you to bow down, that they might walk over you, While you offered your back like the ground, like the street for them to walk on. *Isaiah 51:23*

Hail Mary...

Yet it was our infirmities that he bore, our sufferings that he endured ... he was pierced for our offenses, crushed for our sins... *Isaiah 53:4-5*

Hail Mary...

"They have laid siege against us!" With the rod they strike on the cheek the ruler of Israel. *Micah 4:14*

Hail Mary...

The cords of the nether world enmeshed me, the snares of death overtook me. *2 Samuel 22:6*

Hail Mary...

He shall strike the ruthless with the rod of his mouth, and with the breath of his lips he shall slay the wicked.
Isaiah 11:4

Hail Mary...

Because of his affliction he shall see the light in fullness of days; Through his suffering, my servant shall justify many, and their guilt he shall bear. *Isaiah 53:11*

Hail Mary...

A bruised reed he shall not break, and a smoldering wick he shall not quench, Until he establishes justice on the earth... *Isaiah 42:3-4*

Hail Mary...

He shall bring forth justice to the nations, Not crying out, not shouting, not making his voice heard in the street.
Isaiah 42:1-2

Hail Mary...

In my distress I called upon the LORD and cried out to my God... *2 Samuel 22:7*

Hail Mary...

Glory Be to the Father...

O My Jesus...

Third Sorrowful Mystery
Crowning with Thorns

Though he was harshly treated, he submitted and opened not his mouth; Like a lamb led to the slaughter or a sheep before the shearers, he was silent and opened not his mouth. *Isaiah 53:7*

Our Father...

The waters swirled about me, threatening my life; the abyss enveloped me; seaweed clung about my head. *Jonah 2:6*

Hail Mary...

See, the Lord God is my help; who will prove me wrong? *Isaiah 50:9*

Hail Mary...

But you; Bethlehem-Ephrathah too small to be among the clans of Judah, From you shall come forth for me one who is to be ruler in Israel... *Micah 5:1*

Hail Mary...

Whom have you insulted and blasphemed, against whom have you raised your voice And lifted up your eyes on high? Against the Holy One of Israel! *2 Kings 19:22*

Hail Mary...

For a great King am I, says the LORD of hosts, and my name will be feared among the nations. *Malachi 1:14*

Hail Mary...

His dominion is vast and forever peaceful, From David's throne, and over his kingdom, which he confirms and sustains By judgment and justice, both now and forever. *Isaiah 9:6*

Hail Mary...

And the LORD shall be king over them on Mount Zion, from now on forever. *Micah 4:7*

Hail Mary...

The LORD is true God, he is the living God, the eternal King, Before whose anger the earth quakes, whose wrath the nations cannot endure... *Jeremiah 10:10*

Hail Mary...

I will establish your throne of sovereignty over Israel forever, as I promised your father David... *1 Kings 9:5*

Hail Mary...

I said, "You shall always have someone from your line on the throne of Israel." *1 Kings 9:5*

Hail Mary...

Glory Be to the Father...

O My Jesus...

Fourth Sorrowful Mystery
Carrying of the Cross

Oppressed and condemned, he was taken away, and who would have thought any more of his destiny? *Isaiah 53:8*

> *Our Father...*

They shall look on him whom they have thrust through, and they shall mourn for him as one mourns for an only son... *Zechariah 12:10*

> *Hail Mary...*

They shall grieve over him as one grieves over a first-born. *Zechariah 12:10*

> *Hail Mary...*

Rejoice not over me, O my enemy! though I have fallen, I will arise; though I sit in darkness, the LORD is my light. *Micah 7:8*

> *Hail Mary...*

We will walk in the name of the LORD, our God, forever and ever. *Micah 4:5*

> *Hail Mary...*

When someone falls, does he not rise again? *Jeremiah 8:4*

> *Hail Mary...*

I will strengthen them in the LORD, and they shall walk in his name, says the LORD. *Zechariah 10:12*

> *Hail Mary...*

GOD, my Lord, is my strength; he makes my feet swift
as those of hinds and enables me to go upon the heights.
Habakkuk 3:19

Hail Mary...

He will guard the footsteps of his faithful ones...
1 Samuel 2:9

Hail Mary...

Can a mother forget her infant, be without tenderness
for the child of her womb? *Isaiah 49:15*

Hail Mary...

The God who girded me with strength and kept my way
unerring; Who made my feet swift as those of hinds and
set me on the heights. *2 Samuel 22:33-34*

Hail Mary...

Glory Be to the Father...

O My Jesus...

Fifth Sorrowful Mystery
Crucifixion

He surrendered himself to death and was counted among the wicked; And he shall take away the sins of many, and win pardon for their offenses. *Isaiah 53:12*

Our Father...

But the LORD said to me, "Throw it in the treasury, the handsome price at which they valued me." So I took the thirty pieces of silver and threw them into the treasury... *Zechariah 11:13*

Hail Mary...

The afflicted and the needy seek water in vain, their tongues are parched with thirst. I, the LORD, will answer them; I, the God of Israel, will not forsake them. *Isaiah 41:17*

Hail Mary...

So I became the shepherd of the flock to be slaughtered for the sheep merchants. *Zechariah 11:7*

Hail Mary...

Listen to the petitions of your servant and of your people Israel which they offer in this place. Listen from your heavenly dwelling and grant pardon. *1 Kings 8:30*

Hail Mary...

If he gives his life as an offering for sin, he shall see his descendants in a long life, and the will of the LORD shall be accomplished through him. *Isaiah 53:10*

Hail Mary...

You will cast into the depths of the sea all our sins; You will show faithfulness to Jacob, and grace to Abraham, As you have sworn to our fathers from days of old. *Micah 7:19-20*

Hail Mary...

The LORD roars from Zion, and from Jerusalem raises his voice; The heavens and earth quake, but the LORD is a refuge to his people... *Joel 4:16*

Hail Mary...

The earth quaked and the heavens were shaken, while the clouds sent down showers. Mountains trembled in the presence of the LORD, the One of Sinai. *Judges 5:4-5*

Hail Mary...

You come forth to save your people, to save your anointed one. *Habakkuk 3:13*

Hail Mary...

Listen! the cry of the daughter of my people, far and wide in the land! Is the LORD no longer in Zion is her King no longer in her midst? *Jeremiah 8:19*

Hail Mary...

Glory Be to the Father...

O My Jesus...

Hail Holy Queen...

The Glorious Mysteries

The Sign of the Cross

The Apostle's Creed

For the LORD of hosts will reign on Mount Zion and in Jerusalem, glorious in the sight of his elders.
Isaiah 24:23

Our Father...

I will choose a faithful priest who shall do what I have in heart and mind. I will establish a lasting house for him which shall function in the presence of my anointed one forever. *1 Samuel 2:35*

Hail Mary for Faith

Blessed is the man who trusts in the LORD, whose hope is the Lord. *Jeremiah 17:7*

Hail Mary for Hope

I have loved you, says the LORD; but you say, "How have you loved us?" *Malachi 1:2*

Hail Mary for Charity

Glory Be to the Father...

O My Jesus...

First Glorious Mystery
Resurrection

Rise up in splendor! Your light has come, the glory of
the Lord shines upon you ... nations shall walk by your
light, and kings by your shining radiance. Raise your
eyes and look about; they all gather and come to you.
Isaiah 60:1,3-4

Our Father...

All, from least to greatest, shall know me, says the
LORD, for I will forgive their evildoing and remember
their sin no more. *Jeremiah 31:34*

Hail Mary...

On that day the mourning in Jerusalem shall be as great
as the mourning of Hadadrimmon in the plain of
Megiddo. *Zechariah 12:11*

Hail Mary...

The LORD puts to death and gives life; he casts down to
the nether world, he raises up again. *1 Samuel 2:6*

Hail Mary...

I will turn their mourning into joy, I will console and
gladden them after their sorrows. *Jeremiah 31:13*

Hail Mary...

But the LORD sent a large fish, that swallowed Jonah;
and he remained in the belly of the fish three days and
three nights. *Jonah 2:1*

Hail Mary...

He will revive us after two days; on the third day he will raise us up, to live in his presence. *Hosea 6:2*

Hail Mary...

On that day I will raise up the fallen hut of David; I will wall up its breaches, raise up its ruins and rebuild it as in the days of old. *Amos 9:11*

Hail Mary...

Now will I rise up, says the LORD, now will I be exalted, now be lifted up. *Isaiah 33:10*

Hail Mary...

His splendor spreads like the light; rays shine forth from beside him, where his power is concealed.
Habakkuk 3:4

Hail Mary...

"Therefore will I proclaim you, O LORD, among the nations, and I will sing praise to your name, You who gave great victories to your king and showed kindness to your anointed, to David and his posterity forever."
2 Samuel 22:50-51

Hail Mary...

Glory Be to the Father...

O My Jesus...

Second Glorious Mystery
Ascension

Look down from heaven and regard us from your holy and glorious palace! *Isaiah 63:15*

Our Father...

"I will set up my throne; I will take my seat on the Mount of Assembly, in the recesses of the North. I will ascend above the tops of the clouds; I will be like the Most High!" *Isaiah 14:13-14*

Hail Mary...

Then I heard someone speaking to me from the temple, while the man stood beside me. The voice said to me: Son of man, this is where my throne shall be ... here I will dwell among the Israelites forever. *Ezekiel 43:6-7*

Hail Mary...

Therefore hear the word of the LORD: I saw the LORD seated on his throne, with the whole host of heaven standing by to his right and to his left. *1 Kings 22:19*

Hail Mary...

I saw there the glory of the God of Israel ... the cherubim were stationed to the right of the temple. *Ezekiel 8:4*

Hail Mary...

He shall proclaim peace to the nations. His dominion shall be from sea to sea, and from the River to the ends of the earth. *Zechariah 9:10*

Hail Mary...

No one is like you, O LORD, great are you, great and mighty is your name. Who would not fear you, King of the nations, for it is your due! *Jeremiah 10:6-7*

Hail Mary...

The LORD is exalted, enthroned on high; he fills Zion with right and justice. *Isaiah 33:5*

Hail Mary...

"The Most High in heaven thunders; the LORD judges the ends of the earth. Now may he give strength to his king, and exalt the horn of his anointed!" *1 Samuel 2:10*

Hail Mary...

He has made an eternal covenant with me, set forth in detail and secured. Will he not bring to fruition all my salvation and my every desire? *2 Samuel 23:5*

Hail Mary...

Your house and your kingdom shall endure forever before me, your throne shall stand firm forever.
2 Samuel 7:16

Hail Mary...

Glory Be to the Father...

O My Jesus...

Third Glorious Mystery
Descent of the Holy Spirit

I come to gather nations of every language; they shall come and see my glory. I will set a sign among them; from them I will send fugitives to the nations ... and they shall proclaim my glory among the nations.
Isaiah 66:18-19

Our Father...

God comes from Teman, the Holy One from Mount Paran. Covered are the heavens with his glory, and with his praise the earth is filled. *Habakkuk 3:3*

Hail Mary...

Shall I not open for you the floodgates of heaven, to pour down blessing upon you without measure? *Malachi 3:10*

Hail Mary...

I will pour out on the house of David and on the inhabitants of Jerusalem a spirit of grace and petition...
Zechariah 12:10

Hail Mary...

My spirit which is upon you and my words that I have put into your mouth Shall never leave your mouth, nor the mouths of your children Nor the mouths of your children's children from now on and forever.
Isaiah 59:21

Hail Mary...

I command you: be firm and steadfast! Do not fear nor be dismayed, for the LORD, your God, is with you wherever you go. *Joshua 1:9*

Hail Mary...

Greater will be the future glory of this house than the former, says the LORD of hosts; and in this place I will give peace... *Haggai 2:9*

Hail Mary...

But as for me, I am filled with power, with the spirit of the LORD, with authority and with might. *Micah 3:8*

Hail Mary...

Then afterward I will pour out my spirit upon all mankind. Your sons and daughters shall prophesy, your old men shall dream dreams, your young men shall see visions. *Joel 3:1*

Hail Mary...

"The LORD thundered from heaven; the Most High gave forth his voice." *2 Samuel 22:14*

Hail Mary...

The sun will be turned to darkness, and the moon to blood, At the coming of the day of the LORD, the great and terrible day. Then everyone shall be rescued who calls on the name of the LORD. *Joel 3:4-5*

Hail Mary...

Glory Be to the Father...

O My Jesus...

Fourth Glorious Mystery
Assumption

The favors of the LORD I will recall, the glorious deeds of the Lord, Because of all he has done for us; for he is good to the house of Israel, He has favored us according to his mercy and his great kindness. *Isaiah 63:7*

Our Father...

At that time I will bring you home, and at that time I will gather you; For I will give you renown and praise, among all the peoples of the earth. *Zephaniah 3:20*

Hail Mary...

The LORD has created a new thing upon the earth: the woman must encompass the man with devotion. *Jeremiah 31:22*

Hail Mary...

Shout for joy, O daughter Zion! sing joyfully, O Israel! Be glad and exult with all your heart, O daughter Jerusalem! *Zephaniah 3:14*

Hail Mary...

Say on that day: Give thanks to the LORD, acclaim his name; among the nations make known his deeds, proclaim how exalted is his name. *Isaiah 12:4*

Hail Mary...

Sing to the LORD a new song, his praise from the end of the earth. *Isaiah 42:10*

Hail Mary...

I will make you a light to the nations, that my salvation may reach to the ends of the earth. *Isaiah 49:6*

Hail Mary...

Joy and gladness shall be found in her, thanksgiving and the sound of song. *Isaiah 51:3*

Hail Mary...

I rejoice heartily in the LORD, in my God is the joy of my soul; For he has clothed me with a robe of salvation, and wrapped me in a mantle of justice. *Isaiah 61:10*

Hail Mary...

He will rejoice over you with gladness, and renew you in his love, He will sing joyfully because of you, as one sings at festivals. *Zephaniah 3:17-18*

Hail Mary...

"Toward the faithful you are faithful; toward the wholehearted you are wholehearted; Toward the sincere you are sincere." *2 Samuel 22:26*

Hail Mary...

Glory Be to the Father...

O My Jesus...

Fifth Glorious Mystery
Coronation

Nations shall behold your vindication, and all kings
your glory; You shall be called by a new name
pronounced by the mouth of the LORD. You shall be a
glorious crown in the hand of the LORD, a royal diadem
held by your God. *Isaiah 62:2-3*

Our Father...

For near is the day of the LORD for all the nations! As
you have done, so shall it be done to you, your deed
shall come back upon your own head... *Obadiah 1:15*

Hail Mary...

As the new heavens and the new earth which I will
make Shall endure before me, says the LORD, so shall
your race and your name endure. *Isaiah 66:22*

Hail Mary...

On that day the LORD of hosts will be a glorious crown
And a brilliant diadem to the remnant of his people...
Isaiah 28:5

Hail Mary...

And the LORD, their God, shall save them on that day ...
for they are the jewels in a crown raised aloft over his
land. *Zechariah 9:16*

Hail Mary...

Sing praise to the LORD for his glorious achievement; let
this be known throughout all the earth. *Isaiah 12:5*

Hail Mary...

The lowly will ever find joy in the LORD, and the poor rejoice in the Holy One of Israel. *Isaiah 29:19*

Hail Mary...

Those whom the LORD has ransomed will return and enter Zion singing, crowned with everlasting joy; They will meet with joy and gladness, sorrow and mourning will flee. *Isaiah 35:10*

Hail Mary...

Remember this, O Jacob, you, O Israel, who are my servant! I formed you to be a servant to me; O Israel, by me you shall never be forgotten. *Isaiah 44:21*

Hail Mary...

Look down from heaven and regard us from your holy and glorious palace! *Isaiah 63:15*

Hail Mary...

So shall you summon a nation you knew not, and nations that knew you not shall run to you, Because of the LORD, your God, the Holy One of Israel, who has glorified you. *Isaiah 55:5*

Hail Mary...

Glory Be to the Father...

O My Jesus...

Hail Holy Queen...

My Rock, My Salvation

Psalms 18:3, 31:3, 62:3, 71:3, 89:27, 94:22;
Luke 22:42; John 20:11

BOOK FOUR
The Psalms

I will open my mouth in a parable, I will utter mysteries of old. *Psalms 78:2*

The Our Father Meditation Verses

Selections from the New Testament historical events

The Hail Mary Meditation Verses

Selections from each of the 150 Psalms, in numerical order, corresponding to each of the 150 Hail Marys

The Joyful Mysteries

The Sign of the Cross

The Apostle's Creed

Let me hear sounds of joy and gladness...
Psalms 51:10

Our Father...

The favors of the LORD I will sing forever; through all
generations my mouth shall proclaim your faithfulness.
Psalms 89:2

Hail Mary for Faith

Take courage and be stouthearted, all you who hope in
the LORD. *Psalms 31:25*

Hail Mary for Hope

Love the LORD, all you his faithful ones! *Psalms 31:24*

Hail Mary for Charity

Glory Be to the Father...

O My Jesus...

First Joyful Mystery
Annunciation

Mary said: "I am the servant of the Lord. Let it be done to me as you say." *Luke 1:38*

Our Father...

Happy the man who follows not the counsel of the wicked Nor walks in the way of sinners... but delights in the law of the LORD and meditates on his law day and night. *Psalms 1:1-2*

Hail Mary...

I will proclaim the decree of the LORD: The LORD said to me, "You are my son; this day I have begotten you..." *Psalms 2:7*

Hail Mary...

But you, O LORD, are my shield ... When I call out to the LORD, he answers me from his holy mountain. *Psalms 3:4-5*

Hail Mary...

Know that the LORD does wonders for his faithful one ... You put gladness into my heart... *Psalms 4:4,8*

Hail Mary...

But I, because of your abundant kindness, will enter your house; I will worship at your holy temple... *Psalms 5:8*

Hail Mary...

The LORD has heard my plea; the LORD has accepted my prayer. *Psalms 6:10*

Hail Mary...

I will give thanks to the LORD for his justice, and sing praise to the name of the LORD Most High. *Psalms 7:18*

Hail Mary...

When I behold your heavens, the work of your fingers ... What is man that you should be mindful of him; or the son of man that you should care for him? *Psalms 8:4-5*

Hail Mary...

I will give thanks to you, O LORD, with all my heart; I will declare all your wondrous deeds. *Psalms 9:2*

Hail Mary...

His ways are secure at all times... *Psalms 10:5*

Hail Mary...

Glory Be to the Father...

O My Jesus...

Second Joyful Mystery
Visitation

Elizabeth was filled with the Holy Spirit and cried out in a loud voice: "Blest are you among women and blest is the fruit of your womb." *Luke 1:41-42*

Our Father...

In the LORD I take refuge... "Flee to the mountain like a bird! The LORD is in his holy temple. " *Psalms 11:1,4*

Hail Mary...

"I will grant safety to him who longs for it." The promises of the LORD are sure... You, O LORD, will keep us and preserve us always from this generation. *Psalms 12:6-8*

Hail Mary...

Let my heart rejoice in your salvation; let me sing of the LORD, "He has been good to me." *Psalms 13:6*

Hail Mary...

The LORD looks down from heaven upon the children of men, to see if there be one who is wise and seeks God. Oh, that out of Zion would come the salvation of Israel! *Psalms 14:2,7*

Hail Mary...

Who shall dwell on your holy mountain? He who walks blamelessly and does justice; who thinks the truth in his heart. *Psalms 15:1-2*

Hail Mary...

Therefore my heart is glad and my soul rejoices ... You will show me the path to life, fullness of joys in your presence, the delights at your right hand forever. *Psalms 16:9,11*

Hail Mary...

My steps have been steadfast in your paths, my feet have not faltered. *Psalms 17:5*

Hail Mary...

The LORD rewarded me according to my justice... *Psalms 18:21*

Hail Mary...

The heavens declare the glory of God, and the firmament proclaims his handiwork. *Psalms 19:2*

Hail Mary...

May he grant you what is in your heart and fulfill your every plan. *Psalms 20:5*

Hail Mary...

Glory Be to the Father...

O My Jesus...

Third Joyful Mystery
Nativity

This day in David's city a savior has been born to you, the Messiah and Lord. *Luke 2:11*

Our Father...

For you welcomed him with goodly blessings, you placed on his head a crown of pure gold. He asked life of you: ... For you made him a blessing forever; you gladdened him with the joy of your presence. *Psalms 21:4-5,7*

Hail Mary...

To you I was committed at birth, from my mother's womb you are my God. *Psalms 22:11*

Hail Mary...

The Lord is my shepherd ... Only goodness and kindness follow me all the days of my life; And I shall dwell in the house of the LORD for years to come. *Psalms 23:1,6*

Hail Mary...

Who is this king of glory? The LORD of hosts; he is the king of glory. *Psalms 24:10*

Hail Mary...

To you I lift up my soul, O Lord, my God. In you I trust ... No one who waits for you shall be put to shame. *Psalms 25:1-3*

Hail Mary...

O LORD, I love the house in which you dwell, the tenting-place of your glory. *Psalms 26:8*

Hail Mary...

The LORD is my light and my salvation ... One thing I ask of the LORD; this I seek: To dwell in the house of the LORD all the days of my life, that I may gaze on the loveliness of the LORD... *Psalms 27:1,4*

Hail Mary...

My heart exults, and with my song I give him thanks. *Psalms 28:7*

Hail Mary...

Give to the LORD glory and praise. Give to the LORD the glory due his name; adore the LORD in holy attire. *Psalms 29:1-2*

Hail Mary...

"What gain would there be from my lifeblood, from my going down into the grave?" *Psalms 30:10*

Hail Mary...

Glory Be to the Father...

O My Jesus...

Fourth Joyful Mystery
Presentation

Simeon blessed them and said to Mary his mother: "This child is destined to be the downfall and the rise of many in Israel ... you yourself shall be pierced with a sword..." *Luke 2:34*

Our Father...

Into your hands I commend my spirit; you will redeem me, O LORD, O faithful God. *Psalms 31:6*

Hail Mary...

I will instruct you and show you the way you should walk; I will counsel you, keeping my eye on you. *Psalms 32:8*

Hail Mary...

May your kindness, O LORD, be upon us who have put our hope in you. *Psalms 33:22*

Hail Mary...

He watches over all his bones; not one of them shall be broken. *Psalms 34:21*

Hail Mary...

"I am your salvation." *Psalms 35:3*

Hail Mary...

For with you is the fountain of life, and in your light we see light. *Psalms 36:10*

Hail Mary...

Commit to the LORD your way; trust in him and he will act. *Psalms 37:5*

Hail Mary...

O LORD, all my desire is before you... *Psalms 38:10*

Hail Mary...

Let me know, O LORD, my end and what is the number of my days... *Psalms 39:5*

Hail Mary...

And he put a new song into my mouth, a hymn to our God. Many shall look on in awe and trust in the LORD. *Psalms 40:4*

Hail Mary...

Glory Be to the Father...

O My Jesus...

Fifth Joyful Mystery
Finding in the Temple

He said to them: "Why did you search for me? Did you not know I had to be in my Father's house?" *Luke 2:49*

Our Father...

Let me stand before you forever. *Psalms 41:13*

Hail Mary...

My soul longs for you, O God. *Psalms 42:2*

Hail Mary...

Then will I go in to the altar of God, the God of my gladness and joy... *Psalms 43:4*

Hail Mary...

In God we gloried day by day; your name we praised always. *Psalms 44:9*

Hail Mary...

I will make your name memorable through all generations; therefore shall nations praise you forever and ever. *Psalms 45:18*

Hail Mary...

Come! Behold the deeds of the LORD, the astounding things he has wrought on earth. *Psalms 46:9*

Hail Mary...

He chooses for us our inheritance, the glory of Jacob, whom he loves. *Psalms 47:5*

Hail Mary...

They also see, and at once are stunned ... O God, we ponder your kindness within your temple.
Psalms 48:6,10

Hail Mary...

My mouth shall speak wisdom; prudence shall be the utterance of my heart. *Psalms 49:4*

Hail Mary...

"Gather my faithful ones before me ... Hear, my people, and I will speak..." *Psalms 50:5,7*

Hail Mary...

Glory Be to the Father...

O My Jesus...

Hail Holy Queen...

The Sorrowful Mysteries

The Sign of the Cross

The Apostle's Creed

You do see, for you behold misery and sorrow, taking them in your hands. *Psalms 10:14*

Our Father...

O LORD, hear my prayer; hearken to my pleading in your faithfulness; in your justice answer me. *Psalms 143:1*

Hail Mary for Faith

Why are you so downcast, O my soul? Why do you sigh within me? Hope in God! *Psalms 42:6*

Hail Mary for Hope

The LORD loves those that hate evil... *Psalms 97:10*

Hail Mary for Charity

Glory Be to the Father...

O My Jesus...

First Sorrowful Mystery
Agony in the Garden

In his anguish he prayed with all the greater intensity, and his sweat became like drops of blood falling to the ground. *Luke 22:44*

Our Father...

Have mercy on me, O God, in your goodness; in the greatness of your compassion... *Psalms 51:3*

Hail Mary...

I will thank you always for what you have done, and proclaim the goodness of your name before your faithful ones. *Psalms 52:11*

Hail Mary...

Oh, that out of Zion would come the salvation of Israel! *Psalms 53:7*

Hail Mary...

O God, hear my prayer; hearken to the words of my mouth. *Psalms 54:4*

Hail Mary...

But I will call upon God, and the LORD will save me. In the evening, and at dawn, and at noon, I will grieve and moan, and he will hear my voice. *Psalms 55:17-18*

Hail Mary...

In God, in whose promise I glory, in God I trust without fear; what can flesh do against me? *Psalms 56:5*

Hail Mary...

I call to God the Most High, to God, my benefactor. *Psalms 57:3*

Hail Mary...

He shall bathe his feet in the blood... *Psalms 58:11*

Hail Mary...

Rescue me from my enemies, O my God; from my adversaries defend me. *Psalms 59:2*

Hail Mary...

Give us aid against the foe ... under God we shall do valiantly... *Psalms 60:13-14*

Hail Mary...

Glory Be to the Father...

O My Jesus...

Second Sorrowful Mystery
Scourging

Pilate's next move was to take Jesus and have him scourged. *John 19:1*

Our Father...

Hear, O God, my cry; listen to my prayer!
Psalms 61:2

Hail Mary...

How long will you set upon a man and all together beat him down as though he were a sagging fence, a battered wall? *Psalms 62:4*

Hail Mary...

My soul clings fast to you; your right hand upholds me ... They shall be delivered over to the sword...
Psalms 63:9,11

Hail Mary...

Hear, O God, my voice in my lament; from the dread enemy preserve my life. *Psalms 64:2*

Hail Mary...

We are overcome by our sins; it is you who pardon them. *Psalms 65:4*

Hail Mary...

You laid a heavy burden on our backs. You let men ride over our heads; we went through fire and water...
Psalms 66:11-12

Hail Mary...

So may your way be known upon earth; among all nations, your salvation. *Psalms 67:3*

Hail Mary...

The LORD, my Lord, controls the passageways of death. *Psalms 68:21*

Hail Mary...

Rather they put gall in my food, and in my thirst they gave me vinegar to drink ... But I am afflicted and in pain; let your saving help, O God, protect me. *Psalms 69:22,30*

Hail Mary...

Let them be put to shame and confounded who seek my life. *Psalms 70:3*

Hail Mary...

Glory Be to the Father...

O My Jesus...

Third Sorrowful Mystery
Crowning with Thorns

The soldiers then wove a crown of thorns and fixed it on his head, throwing around his shoulders a cloak of royal purple. *John 19:2*

Our Father...

In you, O LORD, I take refuge; let me never be put to shame. *Psalms 71:1*

Hail Mary...

O God, with your judgment endow the king, and with your justice, the king's son... *Psalms 72:1*

Hail Mary...

I almost lost my balance; my feet all but slipped ... my flesh and my heart waste away. *Psalms 73:2,26*

Hail Mary...

Remember how the fool blasphemes you day after day. *Psalms 74:22*

Hail Mary...

For a cup is in the LORD's hand ... and he pours out from it. *Psalms 75:9*

Hail Mary...

From heaven you made your intervention heard; the earth feared and was silent When God arose for judgment, to save all the afflicted of the earth. *Psalms 76:9-10*

Hail Mary...

Aloud to God I cry; aloud to God, to hear me; on the day of my distress I seek the Lord. *Psalms 77:2-3*

Hail Mary...

He spared them not from death ... and he surrendered his strength into captivity, his glory into the hands of the foe. *Psalms 78:50,61*

Hail Mary...

O LORD, how long? *Psalms 79:5*

Hail Mary...

May your help be with the man of your right hand, with the son of man whom you yourself made strong. *Psalms 80:18*

Hail Mary...

Glory Be to the Father...

O My Jesus...

Fourth Sorrowful Mystery
Carrying of the Cross

Jesus was led away, and carrying the cross by himself, went out to what is called the Place of the Skull.
John 19:17

Our Father...

"I relieved his shoulder of the burden; his hands were freed ... in distress you called, and I rescued you."
Psalms 81:7-8

Hail Mary...

"Yet like men you shall die, and fall like any prince."
Rise, O God. *Psalms 82:7-8*

Hail Mary...

For behold, your enemies raise a tumult, and they who hate you lift up their heads. *Psalms 83:3*

Hail Mary...

The LORD withholds no good thing from those who walk in sincerity. *Psalms 84:12*

Hail Mary...

Justice shall walk before him, and salvation, along the way of his steps. *Psalms 85:14*

Hail Mary...

Incline your ear, O LORD; answer me, for I am afflicted... *Psalms 86:1*

Hail Mary...

And of Zion they shall say: "One and all were born in her; And he who has established her is the Most High LORD." *Psalms 87:5*

Hail Mary...

I am a man without strength ... You have taken my friends away from me... *Psalms 88:5,9*

Hail Mary...

Remember how short my life is; how frail you created all the children of men! *Psalms 89:48*

Hail Mary...

You turn man back to dust... *Psalms 90:3*

Hail Mary...

Glory Be to the Father...

O My Jesus...

Fifth Sorrowful Mystery
Crucifixion

Near the cross of Jesus there stood his mother ... "Now it is finished." Then he bowed his head, and delivered over his spirit. *John 19:25,30*

Our Father...

I will deliver him and glorify him... *Psalms 91:15*

Hail Mary...

It is good ... to proclaim your kindness at dawn and your faithfulness throughout the night. *Psalms 92:2-3*

Hail Mary...

The floods lift up, O LORD, the floods lift up their voice; the floods lift up their tumult. *Psalms 93:3*

Hail Mary...

They attack the life of the just and condemn innocent blood. *Psalms 94:21*

Hail Mary...

In his hands are the depths of the earth. *Psalms 95:4*

Hail Mary...

Tremble before him, all the earth; say among the nations:
The LORD is king. *Psalms 96:9*

Hail Mary...

Clouds and darkness are round about him...
Psalms 97:2

Hail Mary...

His right hand has won victory for him, his holy arm.
The LORD has made his salvation known. *Psalms 98:1-2*

Hail Mary...

The LORD is king; the peoples tremble; he is throned
upon the cherubim; the earth quakes ... a forgiving God
you were to them. *Psalms 99:1,8*

Hail Mary...

Know that the LORD is God; he made us, his we are; his
people, the flock he tends. *Psalms 100:3*

Hail Mary...

Glory Be to the Father...

O My Jesus...

Hail Holy Queen...

The Glorious Mysteries

The Sign of the Cross

The Apostle's Creed

O LORD, our Lord, how glorious is your name over all the earth! Give to the LORD the glory due his name...
Psalms 8:2; 29:2

Our Father...

Mighty are you, O LORD, and your faithfulness surrounds you. *Psalms 89:9*

Hail Mary for Faith

And now, for what do I wait, O LORD? In you is my hope. *Psalms 39:8*

Hail Mary for Hope

The LORD keeps all who love him... *Psalms 145:20*

Hail Mary for Charity

Glory Be to the Father...

O My Jesus...

First Glorious Mystery
Resurrection

Mary Magdalene went to the disciples. "I have seen the Lord!" *John 20:18*

Our Father...

Of kindness and judgment I will sing; to you, O LORD, I will sing praise. *Psalms 101:1*

Hail Mary...

But you, O LORD, abide forever, and your name through all generations. You will arise ...
Psalms 102:13-14

Hail Mary...

The LORD has established his throne in heaven, and his kingdom rules over all. *Psalms 103:19*

Hail Mary...

O LORD, my God, you are great indeed! You are clothed with majesty and glory, robed in light... *Psalms 104:1-2*

Hail Mary...

Give thanks to the LORD, invoke his name; make known among the nations his deeds. *Psalms 105:1*

Hail Mary...

Yet he saved them for his name's sake to make known his power. *Psalms 106:8*

Hail Mary...

Let them give thanks to the LORD for his kindness and his wondrous deeds to the children of men. *Psalms 107:15*

Hail Mary...

Be exalted above the heavens, O God; over all the earth be your glory! *Psalms 108:6*

Hail Mary...

I will speak my thanks earnestly to the LORD, and in the midst of the throng I will praise him... *Psalms 109:30*

Hail Mary...

The LORD said to my Lord: "Sit at my right hand..."
Psalms 110:1

Hail Mary...

Glory Be to the Father...

O My Jesus...

Second Glorious Mystery
Ascension

He was lifted up before their eyes in a cloud which took him from their sight. *Acts of the Apostles 1:9*

Our Father...

He has made known to his people the power of his works... *Psalms 111:6*

Hail Mary...

His horn shall be exalted in glory. *Psalms 112:9*

Hail Mary...

Who is like the LORD, our God, who is enthroned on high and looks upon the heavens and the earth below? *Psalms 113:5-6*

Hail Mary...

Before the face of the Lord, tremble, O earth, before the face of the God of Jacob... *Psalms 114:7*

Hail Mary...

Our God is in heaven; whatever he wills, he does. *Psalms 115:3*

Hail Mary...

How shall I make a return to the LORD for all the good he has done for me? *Psalms 116:12*

Hail Mary...

Praise the LORD, all you nations; glorify him, all you peoples! *Psalms 117:1*

Hail Mary...

Open to me the gates of justice; I will enter them and give thanks to the LORD. *Psalms 118:19*

Hail Mary...

I rejoice at your promise... *Psalms 119:162*

Hail Mary...

All too long have I dwelt with those who hate peace. *Psalms 120:6*

Hail Mary...

Glory Be to the Father...

O My Jesus...

Third Glorious Mystery
Descent of the Holy Spirit

Tongues as of fire appeared, which parted and came to rest on each of them. All were filled with the Holy Spirit. *Acts of the Apostles 2:3-4*

Our Father...

The LORD will guard your coming and your going, both now and forever. *Psalms 121:8*

Hail Mary...

I will say, "Peace be within you!" Because of the house of the LORD, our God, I will pray for your good. *Psalms 122:8-9*

Hail Mary...

To you I lift up my eyes who are enthroned in heaven. *Psalms 123:1*

Hail Mary...

Our help is in the name of the LORD, who made heaven and earth. *Psalms 124:8*

Hail Mary...

Mountains are round about Jerusalem; so the LORD is round about his people, both now and forever. *Psalms 125:2*

Hail Mary...

The LORD has done great things for us; we are glad indeed. *Psalms 126:3*

Hail Mary...

Behold, sons are a gift from the LORD; the fruit of the womb is a reward. *Psalms 127:3*

Hail Mary...

Happy are you who fear the LORD, who walk in his ways! *Psalms 128:1*

Hail Mary...

"The blessing of the LORD be upon you! We bless you in the name of the LORD!" *Psalms 129:8*

Hail Mary...

I trust in the LORD; my soul trusts in his word.
Psalms 130:5

Hail Mary...

Glory Be to the Father...

O My Jesus...

Fourth Glorious Mystery
Assumption

Then Mary said: ..."He has deposed the mighty from their thrones and raised the lowly to high places."
Luke 1:46,52

Our Father...

O LORD, my heart is not proud... I busy not myself with great things, nor with things too sublime for me.
Psalms 131:1

Hail Mary...

In her will I make a horn to sprout for David, I will place a lamp for my anointed. *Psalms 132:17*

Hail Mary...

Behold, how good it is ... for there the LORD has pronounced his blessing, life forever. *Psalms 133:1,3*

Hail Mary...

Lift up your hands toward the sanctuary, and bless the LORD. *Psalms 134:2*

Hail Mary...

He sent signs and wonders into your midst...
Psalms 135:9

Hail Mary...

Give thanks to the God of heaven, for his mercy endures forever. *Psalms 136:26*

Hail Mary...

"Sing for us the songs of Zion!" *Psalms 137:3*

Hail Mary...

The LORD will complete what he has done for me...
Psalms 138:8

Hail Mary...

You knit me in my mother's womb. I give you thanks
that I am fearfully, wonderfully made; wonderful are
your works. *Psalms 139:14*

Hail Mary...

The upright shall dwell in your presence. *Psalms 140:14*

Hail Mary...

Glory Be to the Father...

O My Jesus...

Fifth Glorious Mystery
Coronation

Then Mary said: ..."For he has looked upon his servant in her lowliness; all ages to come shall call me blessed." *Luke 1:46,48*

Our Father...

For toward you, O God, my Lord, my eyes are turned... *Psalms 141:8*

Hail Mary...

Lead me forth ... that I may give thanks to your name. The just shall gather around me when you have been good to me. *Psalms 142:8*

Hail Mary...

I remember the days of old; I meditate on all your doings, the works of your hands I ponder. I stretch out my hands to you. *Psalms 143:5-6*

Hail Mary...

Blessed be the LORD, my rock ... my refuge and fortress, my stronghold, my deliverer, my shield, in whom I trust... *Psalms 144:1-2*

Hail Mary...

Let them discourse of the glory of your kingdom and speak of your might, making known to men your might and the glorious splendor of your kingdom. *Psalms 145:11-12*

Hail Mary...

The LORD raises up those that were bowed down; the LORD loves the just. *Psalms 146:8*

Hail Mary...

Great is our Lord and mighty in power; to his wisdom there is no limit. The LORD sustains the lowly...
Psalms 147:5-6

Hail Mary...

Praise the LORD from the heavens ... Praise him, sun and moon; praise him, all you shining stars. *Psalms 148:1,3*

Hail Mary...

For the LORD loves his people, and he adorns the lowly with victory. Let the faithful exult in glory...
Psalms 149:4-5

Hail Mary...

Praise the LORD in his sanctuary, praise him in the firmament of his strength. Praise him for his mighty deeds ... Let everything that has breath praise the Lord! Alleluia. *Psalms 150:1-2,6*

Hail Mary...

Glory Be to the Father...

O My Jesus...

Hail Holy Queen...

Teacher of Wisdom
Matthew 5:1-12, Luke 2:48-50, 6:20-23

BOOK FIVE
The Blessed Words of Jesus and Mary

"To you the mysteries of the reign of God have been confided ... There is nothing hidden that will not be exposed, nothing concealed that will not be known and brought to light." *Luke 8:10,17*

"Put your trust in God ... I give you my word, if you are ready to believe that you will receive whatever you ask for in prayer, it shall be done for you." *Mark 11:22,24*

The Our Father Meditation Verses

Selections from words spoken by the Blessed Virgin Mary, the Mother of God

The Hail Mary Meditation Verses

Selections from words spoken by Jesus Christ, the Son of God

The Joyful Mysteries

The Sign of the Cross

The Apostle's Creed

"My spirit finds joy in God my savior..." *Luke 1:47*

Our Father...

"Do you believe in the Son of Man?" *John 9:35*

Hail Mary for Faith

"Peace to you ... Why are you disturbed?" *Luke 24:36,38*

Hail Mary for Hope

"You shall love the Lord your God with all your heart, with all your soul, with all your mind, and with all your strength." *Mark 12:30*

Hail Mary for Charity

Glory Be to the Father...

O My Jesus...

First Joyful Mystery
Annunciation

"How can this be since I do not know man?"
Luke 1:34

Our Father...

"Your will be done on earth as it is in heaven."
Matthew 6:10

Hail Mary...

"Fear is useless. What is needed is trust."
Mark 5:36

Hail Mary...

"If you can? Everything is possible to a man who trusts."
Mark 9:23

Hail Mary...

"Put your trust in God." *Mark 11:22*

Hail Mary...

"For man it is impossible, but for God all things are
possible." *Matthew 19:26 [Luke 18:27]*

Hail Mary...

"Because of your faith it shall be done to you."
Matthew 9:29

Hail Mary...

"Whoever does the will of my heavenly Father is ...
mother to me." *Matthew 12:50 [Mark 3:35, Luke 8:20]*

Hail Mary...

"Whoever welcomes me welcomes, not me, but him who sent me." *Mark 9:37 [Matthew 10:40, Luke 9:48]*

Hail Mary...

"A good man produces goodness from the good in his heart... Any sound tree bears good fruit..." *Luke 6:45, Matthew 7:17*

Hail Mary...

"Blest are they who hear the word of God and keep it." *Luke 11:28*

Hail Mary...

Glory be to the Father...

O My Jesus...

Second Joyful Mystery
Visitation

"My being proclaims the greatness of the Lord..."
Luke 1:46

Our Father...

"Go home. It shall be done because you trusted."
Matthew 8:13

Hail Mary...

"Those in Judea must flee to the mountains."
Matthew 24:16 [Mark 13:14, Luke 21:21]

Hail Mary...

"Go home to your family and make it clear to them how much the Lord in his mercy has done for you."
Mark 5:19

Hail Mary...

"I am the light of the world. No follower of mine shall ever walk in darkness; no, he shall possess the light of life." *John 8:12 [John 1:5,9, John 12:46]*

Hail Mary...

"You shall love your neighbor as yourself."
Matthew 22:39 [Mark 12:31, Luke 10:27, John 13:34]

Hail Mary...

"This is how all will know you for my disciples: your love for one another." *John 13:35*

Hail Mary...

"On entering any house, first say, 'Peace to this house.' If there is a peaceable man there, your peace will rest on him, if not, it will come back to you." *Luke 10:5-6*

Hail Mary...

"I solemnly assure you, history has not known a man born of woman greater than John the Baptizer. Yet the least born into the kingdom of God is greater than he." *Matthew 11:11 [Luke 7:28]*

Hail Mary...

"Again I tell you, if two of you join your voices on earth to pray for anything whatever, it shall be granted you by my Father in heaven." *Matthew 18:19 [Luke 11:9, John 15:7]*

Hail Mary...

"Where two or three are gathered in my name, there am I in their midst." *Matthew 18:20*

Hail Mary...

Glory be to the Father...

O My Jesus...

Third Joyful Mystery
Nativity

"He has upheld Israel his servant, ever mindful of his mercy; Even as he promised our fathers, promised Abraham and his descendants forever." *Luke 1:54-55*

Our Father...

"Before Abraham came to be, I AM." *John 8:58*

Hail Mary...

"Indeed, just as the Father possesses life in himself, so has he granted it to the Son to have life in himself." *John 5:26*

Hail Mary...

"Woman, there is your son." *John 19:26*

Hail Mary...

" 'You shall do homage to the Lord your God; him alone shall you adore.' " *Matthew 4:10 [Luke 4:8]*

Hail Mary...

"The Father already loves you, because you have loved me and have believed that I came from God. [I did indeed come from the Father;] I came into the world." *John 16:27-28*

Hail Mary...

"The Son of Man has not come to be served but to serve — to give his life in ransom for the many." *Mark 10:45*

Hail Mary...

"Woman, how does this concern of yours involve me?"
John 2:4

Hail Mary...

"The foxes have lairs, the birds in the sky have nests, but
the Son of Man has nowhere to lay his head."
Matthew 8:20 [Luke 9:58]

Hail Mary...

"Blest are you poor; the reign of God is yours."
Luke 6:20 [Matthew 5:3]

Hail Mary...

"God did not send the Son into the world to condemn
the world, but that the world might be saved through
him." *John 3:17 [John 12:47]*

Hail Mary...

Glory be to the Father...

O My Jesus...

Fourth Joyful Mystery
Presentation

"I am the servant of the Lord." *Luke 1:38*

Our Father...

"The Father and I are one." *John 10:30 [John 14:9]*

Hail Mary...

"We must now go up to Jerusalem so that all that was written by the prophets concerning the Son of Man may be accomplished." *Luke 18:31 [Mark 10:33, Luke 24:44]*

Hail Mary...

"See to it that you tell no one. Go and show yourself to the priest and offer the gift Moses prescribed. That should be the proof they need." *Matthew 8:4 [Luke 5:14, Luke 17:14]*

Hail Mary...

"Anyone who hears my words and puts them into practice is like the wise man who built his house on rock." *Matthew 7:24 [Luke 6:47]*

Hail Mary...

"Do not think that I have come to abolish the law and the prophets. I have come, not to abolish them, but to fulfill them." *Matthew 5:17*

Hail Mary...

"Blest are the eyes that see what you see. I tell you, many prophets and kings wished to see what you see but did not see it, and to hear what you hear but did not hear it." *Luke 10:23-24 [Matthew 13:16-17]*

Hail Mary...

"You must bear witness as well, for you have been with me from the beginning." *John 15:27*

Hail Mary...

" 'The stone which the builders rejected has become the keystone of the structure. It was the Lord who did this and we find it marvelous to behold.' " *Matthew 21:42*

Hail Mary...

"Destroy this temple ... and in three days I will raise it up." *John 2:19*

Hail Mary...

"Have you understood all this?" *Matthew 13:51*

Hail Mary...

Glory be to the Father...

O My Jesus...

Fifth Joyful Mystery
Finding in the Temple

"Son, why have you done this to us? You see that your father and I have been searching for you in sorrow."
Luke 2:48

Our Father...

"Why did you search for me? Did you not know I had to be in my Father's house?" *Luke 2:49*

Hail Mary...

"I have spoken publicly to any who would listen. I always taught in a synagogue or in the temple area where all the Jews come together. There was nothing secret about anything I said." *John 18:20*

Hail Mary...

"You address me as 'Teacher' and 'Lord,' and fittingly enough, for that is what I am." *John 13:13*

Hail Mary...

"It is not to do my will that I have come down from heaven, but to do the will of him who sent me."
John 6:38 [John 4:34]

Hail Mary...

" 'Not on bread alone is man to live but on every utterance that comes from the mouth of God.' "
Matthew 4:4 [Luke 4:4]

Hail Mary...

"To other towns I must announce the good news of the reign of God, because that is why I was sent." *Luke 4:43 [Mark 1:38]*

Hail Mary...

"Go back and report to John what you hear and see: the blind recover their sight, cripples walk, lepers are cured, the deaf hear, dead men are raised to life, and the poor have the good news preached to them."
Matthew 11:4-5

Hail Mary...

"No prophet is without honor except in his native place, among his own kindred, and in his own house." *Mark 6:4 [John 4:44]*

Hail Mary...

" 'My house shall be called a house of prayer,' but you are turning it into 'a den of thieves.' " *Matthew 21:13 [Mark 11:17, Luke 19:46, John 2:16]*

Hail Mary...

"You see these great buildings? Not one stone will be left upon another — all will be torn down."
Mark 13:2 [Matthew 24:2, Luke 21:6]

Hail Mary...

Glory be to the Father...

O My Jesus...

Hail Holy Queen....

The Sorrowful Mysteries

The Sign of the Cross

The Apostle's Creed

"Son ... I have been searching for you in sorrow."
Luke 2:48

Our Father...

"Courage, daughter! Your faith has restored you to
health." *Matthew 9:22*

Hail Mary for Faith

"You are sad for a time, but I shall see you again; then
your hearts will rejoice with a joy no one can take from
you." *John 16:22*

Hail Mary for Hope

"Love your enemy and do good..." *Luke 6:35*

Hail Mary for Charity

Glory Be to the Father...

O My Jesus...

First Sorrowful Mystery
Agony in the Garden

"Let it be done to me as you say." *Luke 1:38*

Our Father...

"The Son of Man is going to be delivered into the hands of men who will put him to death, and he will be raised up on the third day." *Matthew 17:22-23*
[Matthew 20:18-19, Mark 10:33-34, Luke 9:22, Luke 18:33]

Hail Mary...

"You will receive all that you pray for, provided you have faith." *Matthew 21:22 [Matthew 7:7-8]*

Hail Mary...

"Stay here while I go over there and pray."
Matthew 26:36 [Mark 14:32]

Hail Mary...

"My heart is nearly broken with sorrow. Remain here and stay awake with me." *Matthew 26:38 [Mark 14:34]*

Hail Mary...

"My Father, if it is possible, let this cup pass me by. Still, let it be as you would have it, not as I."
Matthew 26:39 [Matthew 26:42, Mark 14:36, Luke 22:42]

Hail Mary...

"Asleep Simeon? You could not stay awake for even an hour?" *Mark 14:37 [Matthew 26:40]*

Hail Mary...

"Be on guard, and pray that you may not undergo the test. The spirit is willing but nature is weak." *Matthew 26:41 [Mark 14:38, Luke 22:40]*

Hail Mary...

"Sleep on now. Enjoy your rest! The hour is on us when the Son of Man is to be handed over to the power of evil men." *Matthew 26:45 [Mark 14:41]*

Hail Mary...

"Get up! Let us be on our way! See, my betrayer is here." *Matthew 26:46 [Mark 14:42]*

Hail Mary...

"Judas, would you betray the Son of Man with a kiss?" *Luke 22:48*

Hail Mary...

Glory be to the Father...

O My Jesus...

Second Sorrowful Mystery
Scourging

"His mercy is from age to age on those who fear him."
Luke 1:50

Our Father...

"Subject us not to the trial but deliver us from the evil
one." *Matthew 6:13 [Luke 11:4]*

Hail Mary...

"Blest too are the sorrowing; they shall be consoled."
Matthew 5:4 [Luke 6:21]

Hail Mary...

"Be on your guard with respect to others. They will hale
you into court, they will flog you in their synagogues.
You will be brought to trial before rulers and kings..."
Matthew 10:17-18 [Mark 13:9, Luke 21:12, John 16:2]

Hail Mary...

"When they hand you over, do not worry about what
you will say or how you will say it. When the hour
comes, you will be given what you are to say."
Matthew 10:19 [Luke 12:11-12]

Hail Mary...

"This is my body ... This is my blood, the blood of the
covenant, to be poured out on behalf of many."
Mark 14:22,24 [Matthew 26:26-28, Luke 22:20]

Hail Mary...

"To you who hear me, I say: Love your enemies, do good to those who hate you; bless those who curse you and pray for those who maltreat you." *Luke 6:27-28*
[Matthew 5:44]

Hail Mary...

"When someone slaps you on one cheek, turn and give him the other..." *Luke 6:29*

Hail Mary...

"Are you saying this on your own, or have others been telling you about me?" *John 18:34*

Hail Mary...

"My kingdom does not belong to this world."
John 18:36

Hail Mary...

"If my kingdom were of this world, my subjects would be fighting to save me from being handed over to the Jews." *John 18:36*

Hail Mary...

Glory be to the Father...

O My Jesus...

Third Sorrowful Mystery
Crowning with Thorns

"He has deposed the mighty from their thrones..."
Luke 1:52

Our Father...

"Blest are you when they insult you and persecute you and utter every kind of slander against you because of me." *Matthew 5:11 [Luke 6:22]*

Hail Mary...

"My command to you is: love your enemies, pray for your persecutors." *Matthew 5:44 [Luke 6:27-28]*

Hail Mary...

"That, I assure you, is why every sin, every blasphemy, will be forgiven men, but blasphemy against the Spirit will not be forgiven." *Matthew 12:31 [Matthew 12:32, Mark 3:28-29, Luke 12:10]*

Hail Mary...

"As it is my kingdom is not here." *John 18:36*

Hail Mary...

"It is you who say I am a king." *John 18:37*

Hail Mary...

"The reason I was born, the reason why I came into the world, is to testify to the truth." *John 18:37*

Hail Mary...

"Anyone committed to the truth hears my voice." *John 18:37*

Hail Mary...

"You yourselves will not be the speakers, the Spirit of your Father will be speaking in you." *Matthew 10:20*

Hail Mary...

"You would have no power over me whatever unless it were given you from above." *John 19:11*

Hail Mary...

"That is why he who handed me over to you is guilty of the greater sin." *John 19:11*

Hail Mary...

Glory be to the Father...

O My Jesus...

Fourth Sorrowful Mystery
Carrying of the Cross

"Do whatever he tells you." *John 2:5*

Our Father...

"Follow me..." *Matthew 8:22*

Hail Mary...

"Come to me, all you who are weary and find life burdensome, and I will refresh you." *Matthew 11:28*

Hail Mary...

"Take my yoke upon your shoulders and learn from me, for I am gentle and humble of heart." *Matthew 11:29*

Hail Mary...

"Your souls will find rest, for my yoke is easy and my burden light." *Matthew 11:29-30*

Hail Mary...

"If a man wishes to come after me, he must deny his very self, take up his cross, and begin to follow in my footsteps." *Matthew 16:24 [Mark 8:34, Luke 9:23]*

Hail Mary...

"The man who holds out to the end, however, is the one who will see salvation." *Matthew 24:13 [Matthew 10:22]*

Hail Mary...

"Daughters of Jerusalem, do not weep for me. Weep for yourselves and for your children." *Luke 23:28*

Hail Mary...

"The days are coming when they will say, 'Happy are the sterile, the wombs that never bore and the breasts that never nursed.' " *Luke 23:29*

Hail Mary...

"Whoever would save his life will lose it, but whoever loses his life for my sake will find it."
Matthew 16:25 [Luke 17:33, John 12:25]

Hail Mary...

"There is no greater love than this: to lay down one's life for one's friends." *John 15:13*

Hail Mary...

Glory be to the Father...

O My Jesus...

Fifth Sorrowful Mystery
Crucifixion

"He has shown might with his arm; he has confused the proud in their inmost thoughts." *Luke 1:51*

Our Father...

"Father, forgive them; they do not know what they are doing." *Luke 23:34*

Hail Mary...

"If you forgive the faults of others, your heavenly Father will forgive you yours." *Matthew 6:14*

Hail Mary...

"My son, your sins are forgiven." *Mark 2:5*
[Luke 5:20, Luke 7:48]

Hail Mary...

"I assure you: this day you will be with me in paradise." *Luke 23:43*

Hail Mary...

"I tell you, there will be the same kind of joy before the angels of God over one repentant sinner." *Luke 15:10*

Hail Mary...

"*Eloi, Eloi lama sabachthani?* ... My God, my God, why have you forsaken me?" *Mark 15:34*

Hail Mary...

"Woman, there is your son ... there is your mother..."
John 19:26,27

Hail Mary...

"I am thirsty ... Now it is finished." *John 19:28,30*

Hail Mary...

"Father, into your hand I commend my spirit."
Luke 23:46

Hail Mary...

"Yes, God so loved the world that he gave his only Son, that whoever believes in him may not die but may have eternal life." *John 3:16*

Hail Mary...

Glory be to the Father...

O My Jesus...

Hail Holy Queen...

The Glorious Mysteries

The Sign of the Cross

The Apostle's Creed

"God who is mighty has done great things for me, holy is his name." *Luke 1:49*

Our Father...

"I tell you, I have never found so much faith among the Israelites ... Your faith has been your salvation."
Luke 7:9,50

Hail Mary for Faith

"I am going where you cannot follow me now; later on you shall come after me." *John 13:36 [John 7:33-34]*

Hail Mary for Hope

"As the Father has loved me, so I have loved you. Live on in my love." *John 15:9*

Hail Mary for Charity

Glory Be to the Father...

O My Jesus...

First Glorious Mystery
Resurrection

"God who is mighty has done great things for me, holy is his name..." *Luke 1:49*

Our Father...

"Just as Jonah spent three days and three nights in the belly of the whale, so will the Son of Man spend three days and three nights in the bowels of the earth." *Matthew 12:40 [Luke 11:30]*

Hail Mary...

"God is not the God of the dead but of the living. All are alive for him." *Luke 20:38 [Matthew 22:32]*

Hail Mary...

"I myself am the living bread come down from heaven. If anyone eats this bread he shall live forever; the bread I will give is my flesh, for the life of the world." *John 6:51*

Hail Mary...

"By pouring this perfume on my body, she has contributed toward my burial preparation. I assure you, wherever the good news is proclaimed throughout the world, what she did will be spoken of as her memorial." *Matthew 26:12-13 [Mark 14:8-9]*

Hail Mary...

"Woman ... why are you weeping? Who is it you are looking for? ... Mary!" *John 20:15-16*

Hail Mary...

"Do not cling to me, for I have not yet ascended to the Father. Rather, go to my brothers and tell them, 'I am ascending to my Father and your Father, to my God and your God!' " *John 20:17*

Hail Mary...

"Peace to you ... Look at my hands and my feet; it is really I. Touch me, and see that a ghost does not have flesh and bones as I do." *Luke 24:36,39*

Hail Mary...

"Take your finger and examine my hands. Put your hand into my side. Do not persist in your unbelief, but believe!" *John 20:27*

Hail Mary...

"You became a believer because you saw me. Blest are they who have not seen and have believed." *John 20:29*

Hail Mary...

"Did I not assure you that if you believed you would see the glory of God displayed?" *John 11:40*

Hail Mary...

Glory be to the Father...

O My Jesus...

Second Glorious Mystery
Ascension

"He has ... raised the lowly to high places." *Luke 1:52*

Our Father...

"Blest are those persecuted for holiness' sake; the reign of God is theirs." *Matthew 5:10*

Hail Mary...

"Go back home and recount all that God has done for you." *Luke 8:39*

Hail Mary...

"I — once I am lifted up from earth — will draw all men to myself." *John 12:32*

Hail Mary...

"I am going where you cannot follow me now; later on you shall come after me." *John 13:36 [John 7:33-34]*

Hail Mary...

"Our Father in heaven, hallowed be your name, your kingdom come..." *Matthew 6:9-10 [Luke 11:2]*

Hail Mary...

"No one knows the Son but the Father, and no one knows the Father but the Son — and anyone to whom the Son wishes to reveal him." *Matthew 11:27 [John 6:46]*

Hail Mary...

"I have given you glory on earth by finishing the work you gave me to do." *John 17:4*

Hail Mary...

"Do you now, Father, give me glory at your side, a glory I had with you before the world began." *John 17:5*

Hail Mary...

"The Son of Man will come with his Father's glory accompanied by his angels. When he does, he will repay each man according to his conduct."
Matthew 16:27 [Matthew 24:30, Mark 13:26, Mark 14:62]

Hail Mary...

"Your heavenly Father knows all that you need. Seek first his kingship over you, his way of holiness, and all these things will be given you besides."
Matthew 6:32-33

Hail Mary...

Glory be to the Father...

O My Jesus...

Third Glorious Mystery
Descent of the Holy Spirit

"My spirit finds joy in God my savior..." *Luke 1:47*

Our Father...

"It is much better for you that I go. If I fail to go, the
Paraclete will never come to you, whereas if I go, I will
send him to you." *John 16:7 [John 14:16]*

Hail Mary...

"John baptized with water, but within a few days you
will be baptized with the Holy Spirit."
Acts of the Apostles 1:5

Hail Mary...

"You will receive power when the Holy Spirit comes
down on you; then you are to be my witnesses in
Jerusalem, throughout Judea and Samaria, yes, even to
the ends of the earth." *Acts of the Apostles 1:8*

Hail Mary...

"In that hour, say what you are inspired to say. It will
not be yourselves speaking but the Holy Spirit."
Mark 13:11

Hail Mary...

"God is Spirit, and those who worship him must worship
in Spirit and truth." *John 4:24*

Hail Mary...

"Teach them to carry out everything I have commanded you. And know that I am with you always, until the end of the world!" *Matthew 28:20*

Hail Mary...

"You are witnesses of this. See, I send down upon you the promise of my Father. Remain here in the city until you are clothed with power from on high."
Luke 24:48-49

Hail Mary...

"I solemnly assure you, no one can enter into God's kingdom without being begotten of water and Spirit."
John 3:5

Hail Mary...

"Go into the whole world and proclaim the good news to all creation. The man who believes in it and accepts baptism will be saved..." *Mark 16:15-16*

Hail Mary...

"Go, therefore, and make disciples of all the nations. Baptize them in the name 'of the Father, and of the Son, and of the Holy Spirit.' " *Matthew 28:19*

Hail Mary...

Glory be to the Father...

O My Jesus...

Fourth Glorious Mystery
Assumption

"He has ... raised the lowly to high places. *Luke 1:52*

Our Father...

"There is your mother." *John 19:27*

Hail Mary...

"Blest are the single-hearted for they shall see God."
Matthew 5:8

Hail Mary...

"He who acts in truth comes into the light, to make clear
that his deeds are done in God." *John 3:21*

Hail Mary...

"I solemnly assure you, the man who hears my word and
has faith in him who sent me possesses eternal life."
John 5:24

Hail Mary...

"If a man is true to my word he shall never see death."
John 8:51

Hail Mary...

"I am the resurrection and the life: whoever believes in
me, though he should die, will come to life; and whoever
is alive and believes in me will never die." *John 11:25-26*

Hail Mary...

"You are not far from the reign of God." *Mark 12:34*

Hail Mary...

"Do not lay up for yourselves an earthly treasure ...
Make it your practice instead to store up heavenly
treasure..." *Matthew 6:19-20*

Hail Mary...

"I want you to observe that this poor widow contributed
more than all the others who donated to the treasury."
Mark 12:43 [Luke 21:4]

Hail Mary...

"I know them, and they follow me. I give them eternal
life, and they shall never perish." *John 10:27-28*

Hail Mary...

Glory be to the Father...

O My Jesus...

Fifth Glorious Mystery
Coronation

"He has looked upon his servant in her lowliness; all ages to come shall call me blessed." *Luke 1:48*

Our Father...

" 'You shall love the Lord your God with your whole heart, with your whole soul, and with all your mind.' " *Matthew 22:37 [Mark 12:30]*

Hail Mary...

"Since I know that his commandment means eternal life, whatever I say is spoken just as he instructed me." *John 12:50*

Hail Mary...

"Be glad and rejoice, for your reward is great in heaven." *Matthew 5:12 [Luke 6:23]*

Hail Mary...

"Your light must shine before men so that they may see goodness in your acts and give praise to your heavenly Father." *Matthew 5:16*

Hail Mary...

"You must be made perfect as your heavenly Father is perfect." *Matthew 5:48*

Hail Mary...

"As the Father has loved me, so I have loved you. Live on in my love." *John 15:9*

Hail Mary...

"The saints will shine like the sun in their Father's kingdom. Let everyone heed what he hears!"
Matthew 13:43

Hail Mary...

"Whoever exalts himself shall be humbled, but whoever humbles himself shall be exalted." *Matthew 23:12*

Hail Mary...

"Whoever makes himself lowly, becoming like this child, is of greatest importance in that heavenly reign."
Matthew 18:4 [Mark 10:15, Luke 18:17]

Hail Mary...

"I offer you praise, O Father, Lord of heaven and earth, because what you have hidden from the learned and the clever you have revealed to the merest children."
Luke 10:21 [Matthew 11:25]

Hail Mary...

Glory be to the Father...

O My Jesus...

Hail Holy Queen...

Magnificat

Luke 1:47,52, Romans 16:6

BOOK SIX
Sts Peter and Paul

At every opportunity pray in the Spirit, using prayers and petitions of every sort. Pray constantly and attentively for all in the holy company. Pray for me that God may put his word on my lips, that I may courageously make known the mystery of the gospel.
Ephesians 6:18-19

The Our Father Meditation Verses

Selections from 1 Peter and 2 Peter

The Hail Mary Meditation Verses

Selections from the Epistles of St Paul — Colossians, 1 Corinthians, 2 Corinthians, Ephesians, Galatians, Philemon, Philippians, Romans, 1 Thessalonians, 2 Thessalonians, 1 Timothy, 2 Timothy, Titus

The Joyful Mysteries

The Sign of the Cross

The Apostle's Creed

May grace be yours and peace in abundance through your knowledge of God and of Jesus, our Lord. *2 Peter 1:2*

Our Father...

Use the faith you have as your rule of life in the sight of God. *Romans 14:22*

Hail Mary for Faith

Hoping against hope, Abraham believed and so became the father of many nations, just as it was once told him, "Numerous as this shall your descendants be." *Romans 4:18*

Hail Mary for Hope

Your love must be sincere. Detest what is evil, cling to what is good. Love one another with the affection of brothers. *Romans 12:9-10*

Hail Mary for Charity

Glory Be to the Father...

O My Jesus...

First Joyful Mystery
Annunciation

Remain calm so that you will be able to pray ... As generous distributors of God's manifold grace, put your gifts at the service of one another, each in the measure he has received. *1 Peter 4:7,10*

Our Father...

What we utter is God's wisdom: a mysterious, a hidden wisdom. God planned it before all ages for our glory. *1 Corinthians 2:7*

Hail Mary...

Those whom he foreknew he predestined to share the image of his Son, that the Son might be the first-born of many brothers. *Romans 8:29*

Hail Mary...

In him you too were chosen; when you heard the glad tidings of salvation, the word of truth, and believed in it, you were sealed with the Holy Spirit who had been promised. *Ephesians 1:13*

Hail Mary...

God has fashioned us for this very thing and has given us the Spirit as a pledge of it. *2 Corinthians 5:5*

Hail Mary...

You must realize that, when you offer yourselves to someone as obedient slaves, you are the slaves of the one you obey ... which leads to justice. *Romans 6:16*

Hail Mary...

Just as through one man's disobedience all became sinners, so through one man's obedience all shall become just. *Romans 5:19*

Hail Mary...

Your obedience is known to all, and so I am delighted with you. I want you to be wise in regard to what is good and innocent of all evil. *Romans 16:19*

Hail Mary...

In him we were chosen; for in the decree of God, who administers everything according to his will and counsel, we were predestined to praise his glory by being the first to hope in Christ. *Ephesians 1:11-12*

Hail Mary...

The virgin ... is concerned with things of the Lord, in pursuit of holiness in body and spirit. *1 Corinthians 7:34*

Hail Mary...

You must know that your body is a temple of the Holy Spirit, who is within — the Spirit you have received from God. *1 Corinthians 6:19*

Hail Mary...

Glory Be to the Father...

O My Jesus...

Second Joyful Mystery
Visitation

By observing your good works they may give glory to God on the day of visitation ... Greet one another with the embrace of true love. Peace to all of you who are in Christ. *1 Peter 2:12; 1 Peter 5:14*

Our Father...

We walk by faith, not by sight ... "How beautiful are the feet of those who announce good news!" *2 Corinthians 5:7; Romans 10:15*

Hail Mary...

Greet one another with a holy kiss. All the holy ones send greetings to you. *2 Corinthians 13:12*

Hail Mary...

Rejoice always, never cease praying, render constant thanks; such is God's will for you in Christ Jesus. *1 Thessalonians 5:16-18*

Hail Mary...

And may the Lord increase you and make you overflow with love for one another and for all, even as our love does for you. *1 Thessalonians 3:12*

Hail Mary...

Encourage one another. Live in harmony and peace, and the God of love and peace will be with you. *2 Corinthians 13:11*

Hail Mary...

Look on the needs of the saints as your own; be generous in offering hospitality. *Romans 12:13*

Hail Mary...

Because you are God's chosen ones, holy and beloved, clothe yourselves with heartfelt mercy, with kindness, humility, meekness, and patience. *Colossians 3:12*

Hail Mary...

Each should please his neighbor so as to do him good by building up his spirit. *Romans 15:2*

Hail Mary...

While we have the opportunity, let us do good to all men — but especially those of the household of the faith.
Galatians 6:10

Hail Mary...

Out of love, place yourselves at one another's service ...
"You shall love your neighbor as yourself."
Galatians 5:13-14

Hail Mary...

Glory Be to the Father...

O My Jesus...

Third Joyful Mystery
Nativity

Praised be the God and Father of our Lord Jesus Christ, he who in his great mercy gave us new birth; a birth unto hope ... a birth to an imperishable inheritance ... a birth to a salvation... *1 Peter 1:3-5*

Our Father...

Pay each one his due: taxes to whom taxes are due; toll to whom toll is due; respect and honor to everyone who deserves them. *Romans 13:7*

Hail Mary...

She will be saved through childbearing, provided she continues in faith and love and holiness — her chastity being taken for granted. *1 Timothy 2:15*

Hail Mary...

The proof that you are sons is the fact that God has sent forth into our hearts the spirit of his Son which cries out "Abba!" *Galatians 4:6*

Hail Mary...

God sent forth His Son born of a woman, born under the law, to deliver from the law those who were subjected to it, so that we might receive our status as adopted sons. *Galatians 4:4-5*

Hail Mary...

He emptied himself and took the form of a slave, being born in the likeness of men ... Because of this, God highly exalted him and bestowed on him the name above every other name... *Philippians 2:7,9*

Hail Mary...

"Out of Zion will come the deliverer who shall remove all impiety from Jacob; and this is the covenant I will make with them when I take away their sins." *Romans 11:26-27*

Hail Mary...

Falling prostrate, he will worship God, crying out, "God is truly among you." *1 Corinthians 14:25*

Hail Mary...

Love ... springs from a pure heart, a good conscience, and sincere faith. *1 Timothy 1:5*

Hail Mary...

The grace of God has appeared, offering salvation to all men ... He saved us through the baptism of new birth and renewal by the Holy Spirit. *Titus 2:11; 3:5*

Hail Mary...

If you belong to Christ you are descendants of Abraham, which means you inherit all that was promised. *Galatians 3:29*

Hail Mary...

Glory Be to the Father...

O My Jesus...

Fourth Joyful Mystery
Presentation

By obedience to the truth you have purified yourselves for a genuine love of your brothers; therefore, love one another constantly from the heart. *1 Peter 1:22*

Our Father...

The man who observes the day does so to honor the Lord. *Romans 14:6*

Hail Mary...

Let everyone obey the authorities that are over him, for there is no authority except from God, and all authority that exists is established by God. *Romans 13:1*

Hail Mary...

Is it because you observe the law or because you have faith in what you heard that God lavishes the Spirit on you and works wonders in your midst? *Galatians 3:5*

Hail Mary...

Yet the law is holy and the commandment is holy and just and good. *Romans 7:12*

Hail Mary...

We have been praying for you unceasingly and asking that you may attain full knowledge of his will through perfect wisdom and spiritual insight. *Colossians 1:9*

Hail Mary...

Your faith rests not on the wisdom of men but on the power of God. *1 Corinthians 2:5*

Hail Mary...

The prophet ... speaks to men for their upbringing, their encouragement, their consolation. *1 Corinthians 14:3*

Hail Mary...

God has given us the wisdom to understand fully the mystery, the plan he was pleased to decree in Christ, to be carried out in the fullness of time... *Ephesians 1:9-10*

Hail Mary...

Whatever you do — you should do all for the glory of God. *1 Corinthians 10:31*

Hail Mary...

While we live we are responsible to the Lord... *Romans 14:8*

Hail Mary...

Glory Be to the Father...

O My Jesus...

Fifth Joyful Mystery
Finding in the Temple

Grow rather in grace, and in the knowledge of our Lord and Savior Jesus Christ. Glory be to him now and to the day of eternity! *2 Peter 3:18*

Our Father...

Are you not aware that you are the temple of God, and that the Spirit of God dwells in you? *1 Corinthians 3:16*

Hail Mary...

Let the word of Christ, rich as it is, dwell in you. In wisdom made perfect, instruct and admonish one another. *Colossians 3:16*

Hail Mary...

Use the faith you have as your rule of life in the sight of God. *Romans 14:22*

Hail Mary...

Your teaching must have the integrity of serious, sound words to which no one can take exception. *Titus 2:8*

Hail Mary...

What thanks can we give to God for all the joy we feel in his presence. *1 Thessalonians 3:9*

Hail Mary...

You will lead a life worthy of the Lord and pleasing to him in every way. You will multiply good works of every sort and grow in the knowledge of God. *Colossians 1:10*

Hail Mary...

"Honor your father and mother" is the first commandment to carry a promise with it — "that it may go well with you, and that you may have long life on the earth." *Ephesians 6:2,3*

Hail Mary...

How deep are the riches and the wisdom and the knowledge of God! How inscrutable his judgments, how unsearchable his ways! *Romans 11:33*

Hail Mary...

Children, obey your parents in the Lord, for that is what is expected of you. *Ephesians 6:1*

Hail Mary...

Fathers ... bring them up with the training and instruction befitting the Lord. *Ephesians 6:4*

Hail Mary...

Glory Be to the Father...

O My Jesus...

Hail Holy Queen...

The Sorrowful Mysteries

The Sign of the Cross

The Apostle's Creed

You may for a time have to suffer the distress of many trials... *1 Peter 1:6*

Our Father...

Faith, then, comes through hearing, and what is heard is the word of Christ. *Romans 10:17*

Hail Mary for Faith

This explains why we work and struggle as we do; our hopes are fixed on the living God who is the savior of all men, but especially of those who believe.
1 Timothy 4:10

Hail Mary for Hope

Love is patient; love is kind ... Love never fails.
1 Corinthians 13:4,8

Hail Mary for Charity

Glory Be to the Father...

O My Jesus...

First Sorrowful Mystery
Agony in the Garden

Let those who suffer as God's will requires continue in good deeds, and entrust their lives to a faithful Creator. *1 Peter 4:19*

Our Father...

Is not the cup of blessing we bless a sharing in the blood of Christ? And is not the bread we break a sharing in the body of Christ? *1 Corinthians 10:16*

Hail Mary...

Pray perseveringly, be attentive to prayer, and pray in a spirit of thanksgiving. *Colossians 4:2*

Hail Mary...

We know that all creation groans and is in agony even until now. *Romans 8:22*

Hail Mary...

He comforts us in all our afflictions and thus enables us to comfort those who are in trouble, with the same consolation we have received from him.
2 Corinthians 1:4

Hail Mary...

We groan while we are here, even as we yearn to have our heavenly habitation envelop us. *2 Corinthians 5:2*

Hail Mary...

The Spirit too helps us in our weakness, for we do not know how to pray as we ought; but the Spirit himself makes intercession for us with groanings which cannot be expressed in speech. *Romans 8:26*

Hail Mary...

Dismiss all anxiety from your minds. Present your needs to God in every form of prayer and in petitions full of gratitude. *Philippians 4:6*

Hail Mary...

Pray that we may be delivered from confused and evil men ... In the Lord we are confident that you are doing and will continue to do whatever we enjoin.
2 Thessalonians 3:2,4

Hail Mary...

The night is far spent; the day draws near. Let us cast off deeds of darkness and put on the armor of light.
Romans 13:12

Hail Mary...

When we were still with you, we used to warn you that we would undergo trial; now it has happened, and you know what we meant. *1 Thessalonians 3:4*

Hail Mary...

Glory Be to the Father...

O My Jesus...

Second Sorrowful Mystery
Scourging

Do not return evil for evil or insult for insult. Return a
blessing instead. This you have been called to do, that
you may receive a blessing as your inheritance.
1 Peter 3:9

Our Father...

Is it possible that he who did not spare his own Son but
handed him over for the sake of us all will not grant us
all things besides? *Romans 8:32*

Hail Mary...

If we are afflicted it is for your encouragement and
salvation, and when we are consoled it is for your
consolation, so that you may endure patiently the same
sufferings we endure. *2 Corinthians 1:6*

Hail Mary...

And hoping for what we cannot see means awaiting it
with patient endurance. *Romans 8:25*

Hail Mary...

Five times at the hands of the Jews I received forty lashes
less one; three times I was beaten with rods...
2 Corinthians 11:24-25

Hail Mary...

What a wretched man I am! Who can free me from this
body under the power of death? *Romans 7:24*

Hail Mary...

In all circumstances hold faith up before you as your shield; it will help you extinguish the fiery darts of the evil one. *Ephesians 6:16*

Hail Mary...

Be steadfast and persevering, my beloved brothers, fully engaged in the work of the Lord. You know that your toil is not in vain when it is done in the Lord. *1 Corinthians 15:58*

Hail Mary...

We know that affliction makes for endurance, and endurance for tested virtue, and tested virtue for hope. *Romans 5:3-4*

Hail Mary...

And this hope will not leave us disappointed, because the love of God has been poured out in our hearts through the Holy Spirit who has been given to us. *Romans 5:5*

Hail Mary...

The Lord will continue to rescue me from all attempts to do me harm and will bring me safe to his heavenly kingdom. *2 Timothy 4:18*

Hail Mary...

Glory Be to the Father...

O My Jesus...

Third Sorrowful Mystery
Crowning with Thorns

Do not be surprised, beloved, that a trial by fire is
occurring in your midst ... Consider that our Lord's
patience is directed toward salvation.
1 Peter 4:12; 2 Peter 3:15

Our Father...

We are weighed down because we do not wish to be
stripped naked but rather to have the heavenly dwelling
envelop us, so that what is mortal may be absorbed by
life. *2 Corinthians 5:4*

Hail Mary...

Whom would you say I am trying to please at this point
— men or God? Is this how I seek to ingratiate myself
with men? *Galatians 1:10*

Hail Mary...

Who shall bring a charge against God's chosen ones?
God, who justifies? *Romans 8:33*

Hail Mary...

Bless your persecutors; bless and do not curse them.
Romans 12:14

Hail Mary...

We were crushed beyond our strength, even to the point
of despairing of life. We were left to feel like men
condemned to death so that we might trust, not in
ourselves, but in God who raises the dead.
2 Corinthians 1:8-9

Hail Mary...

Rejoice in hope, be patient under trial, persevere in prayer. *Romans 12:12*

Hail Mary...

Draw your strength from the Lord and his mighty power. *Ephesians 6:10*

Hail Mary...

If God is for us, who can be against us? *Romans 8:31*

Hail Mary...

Then God sent his Son in the likeness of sinful flesh as a sin offering ... so that the just demands of the law might be fulfilled in us... *Romans 8:3-4*

Hail Mary...

"In an acceptable time I have heard you, on a day of salvation I have helped you." Now is the acceptable time! Now is the day of salvation! *2 Corinthians 6:2*

Hail Mary...

Glory Be to the Father...

O My Jesus...

Fourth Sorrowful Mystery
Carrying of the Cross

Who indeed can harm you if you are committed deeply to doing what is right? Even if you should have to suffer for justice' sake, happy will you be. *1 Peter 3:13-14*

Our Father...

The punishment already inflicted by the majority on such a one is enough; you should now relent and support him so that he may not be crushed by too great a weight of sorrow. *2 Corinthians 2:6-7*

Hail Mary...

"For your sake we are being slain all the day long; we are looked upon as sheep to be slaughtered." *Romans 8:36*

Hail Mary...

We are persecuted but never abandoned; we are struck down but never destroyed. *2 Corinthians 4:9*

Hail Mary...

I further ask, does their stumbling mean that they are forever fallen? Not at all! *Romans 11:11*

Hail Mary...

There is no limit to love's forbearance, to its trust, its hope, its power to endure. *1 Corinthians 13:7*

Hail Mary...

I consider the sufferings of the present to be as nothing
compared with the glory to be revealed in us.
Romans 8:18

Hail Mary...

We are afflicted in every way possible, but we are not
crushed; full of doubts, we never despair.
2 Corinthians 4:8

Hail Mary...

We ourselves, although we have the Spirit as first fruits,
groan inwardly while we await the redemption of our
bodies. In hope we were saved. *Romans 8:23-24*

Hail Mary...

In him who is the source of my strength I have strength
for everything. *Philippians 4:13*

Hail Mary...

The present burden of our trial is light enough, and
earns for us an eternal weight of glory beyond all
comparison. *2 Corinthians 4:17*

Hail Mary...

Glory Be to the Father...

O My Jesus...

Fifth Sorrowful Mystery
Crucifixion

Realize that you were delivered ... by Christ's blood
beyond all price: the blood of a spotless, unblemished
lamb chosen before the world's foundation...
1 Peter 1:18-20

> *Our Father...*

He was known to be of human estate, and it was thus
that he humbled himself, obediently accepting even
death, death on a cross! *Philippians 2:8*

> *Hail Mary...*

Through his blood, God made him the means of
expiation for all who believe. *Romans 3:25*

> *Hail Mary...*

I beg you through the mercy of God to offer your bodies
as a living sacrifice holy and acceptable to God...
Romans 12:1

> *Hail Mary...*

It is precisely in this that God proves his love for us: that
while we were still sinners, Christ died for us.
Romans 5:8

> *Hail Mary...*

Faith in the heart leads to justification, confession on the
lips to salvation. Scripture says, "No one who believes in
him will be put to shame." *Romans 10:10-11*

> *Hail Mary...*

We have put our hope in him who will never cease to deliver us. *2 Corinthians 1:10*

Hail Mary...

Just as a single offense brought condemnation to all men, a single righteous act brought all men acquittal and life. *Romans 5:18*

Hail Mary...

It is in Christ and through his blood that we have been redeemed and our sins forgiven, so immeasurably generous is God's favor to us. *Ephesians 1:7-8*

Hail Mary...

There are in the end three things that last: faith, hope, and love, and the greatest of these is love. *1 Corinthians 13:13*

Hail Mary...

Do everything with love. *1 Corinthians 16:14*

Hail Mary...

Glory Be to the Father...

O My Jesus...

Hail Holy Queen...

The Glorious Mysteries

The Sign of the Cross

The Apostle's Creed

The God of all grace, who called you to his everlasting glory in Christ, will himself restore, confirm, strengthen, and establish those who have suffered a little while. *1 Peter 5:10*

Our Father...

Because of your praiseworthy service they are glorifying God for your obedient faith in the gospel of Christ, and for your generosity in sharing with them and with all. *2 Corinthians 9:13*

Hail Mary for Faith

Hope is not hope if its object is seen; how is it possible for one to hope for what he sees? *Romans 8:24*

Hail Mary for Hope

God is rich in mercy; because of his great love for us. *Ephesians 2:4*

Hail Mary for Charity

Glory Be to the Father...

O My Jesus...

First Glorious Mystery
Resurrection

This is the salvation which the prophets carefully
searched out and examined. They prophesied the divine
favor that was destined to be yours ... the sufferings
destined for Christ and the glories that would follow.
1 Peter 1:10-11

Our Father...

For our faith will be credited to us also if we believe in
him who raised Jesus our Lord from the dead, the Jesus
who was handed over to death for our sins and raised
up for our justification. *Romans 4:24-25*

Hail Mary...

Christ died for our sins in accordance with the Scriptures
... was buried ... rose on the third day ... was seen by
Cephas, then by the twelve. *1 Corinthians 15:3-5*

Hail Mary...

Through baptism into his death we were buried with
him, so that, just as Christ was raised from the dead by
the glory of the Father, we too might live a new life.
Romans 6:4

Hail Mary...

God's gifts and his call are irrevocable. *Romans 11:29*

Hail Mary...

We know that God makes all things work together for
the good of those who have been called according to his
decree. *Romans 8:28*

Hail Mary...

For if, when we were God's enemies, we were reconciled to him by the death of his Son, it is all the more certain that we who have been reconciled will be saved by his life. *Romans 5:10*

Hail Mary...

It is true he was crucified out of weakness, but he lives by the power of God. *2 Corinthians 13:4*

Hail Mary...

All men are now undeservedly justified by the gift of God, through redemption wrought in Christ Jesus. *Romans 3:24*

Hail Mary...

Just as in Adam all die, so in Christ all will come to life again, but each one in proper order: Christ the first fruits and then, at his coming, all those who belong to him. *1 Corinthians 15:22-23*

Hail Mary...

This means that if anyone is in Christ, he is a new creation. The old order has passed away; now all is new! *2 Corinthians 5:17*

Hail Mary...

Glory Be to the Father...

O My Jesus...

Second Glorious Mystery
Ascension

He received glory and praise from God the Father when that unique declaration came to him out of the majestic splendor: "This is my beloved Son, on whom my favor rests." *2 Peter 1:17*

Our Father...

Both in life and in death we are the Lord's. That is why Christ died and came to life again, that he might be Lord of both the dead and the living. *Romans 14:8-9*

Hail Mary...

We do not fix our gaze on what is seen but on what is unseen. What is seen is transitory; what is unseen lasts forever. *2 Corinthians 4:18*

Hail Mary...

It is like the strength he showed in raising Christ from the dead and seating him at his right hand in heaven, high above every principality, power, virtue, and domination, and every name that can be given in this age or in the age to come. *Ephesians 1:19-21*

Hail Mary...

He has put all things under Christ's feet and has made him, thus exalted, head of the church... *Ephesians 1:22*

Hail Mary...

"He ascended" — what does this mean but that he had first descended into the lower regions of the earth? He who descended is the very one who ascended high above the heavens, that he might fill all men with his gifts. *Ephesians 4:9-10*

Hail Mary...

"As surely as I live, says the Lord, every knee shall bend before me and every tongue shall give praise to God." *Romans 14:11*

Hail Mary...

So that at Jesus' name every knee must bend in the heavens, on the earth, and under the earth, and every tongue proclaim to the glory of God the Father: JESUS CHRIST IS LORD! *Philippians 2:10-11*

Hail Mary...

His death was death to sin, once for all; his life is life for God. *Romans 6:10*

Hail Mary...

Through him we have gained access by faith to the grace in which we now stand, and we boast of our hope for the glory of God. *Romans 5:2*

Hail Mary...

To the King of ages, the immortal, the invisible, the only God, be honor and glory forever and ever! *1 Timothy 1:17*

Hail Mary...

Glory Be to the Father...

O My Jesus...

Third Glorious Mystery
Descent of the Holy Spirit

That divine power of his has freely bestowed on us
everything necessary for a life of genuine piety, through
knowledge of him who called us by his glory and power.
2 Peter 1:3

Our Father...

God is the one who firmly establishes us along with you
in Christ; it is he who anointed us and has sealed us,
thereby depositing the first payment, the Spirit, in our
hearts. *2 Corinthians 1:21-22*

Hail Mary...

All of us, gazing on the Lord's glory with unveiled faces,
are being transformed from glory to glory into his very
image by the Lord who is the Spirit. *2 Corinthians 3:18*

Hail Mary...

Be filled with the Spirit, addressing one another in
psalms and hymns and inspired songs. Sing praise to
the Lord with all your hearts. *Ephesians 5:18-19*

Hail Mary...

The Spirit we have received is not the world's spirit but
God's Spirit, helping us to recognize the gifts he has
given us. *1 Corinthians 2:12*

Hail Mary...

The fruit of the spirit is love, joy, peace, patient endurance, kindness, generosity, faith, mildness, and chastity. *Galatians 5:22-23*

Hail Mary...

To each person the manifestation of the Spirit is given for the common good. To one the Spirit gives wisdom in discourse, to another the power to express knowledge. *1 Corinthians 12:7-8*

Hail Mary...

Through the Spirit one receives faith. *1 Corinthians 12:9*

Hail Mary...

My prayer is that your sharing of the faith with others may enable you to know all the good which is ours in Christ. *Philemon 1:6*

Hail Mary...

God has revealed this wisdom to us through the Spirit. The Spirit scrutinizes all matters, even the deep things of God. *1 Corinthians 2:10*

Hail Mary...

The Spirit God has given us is no cowardly spirit, but rather one that makes us strong, loving and wise. Therefore, never be ashamed of your testimony to our Lord... *2 Timothy 1:7-8*

Hail Mary...

Glory Be to the Father...

O My Jesus...

Fourth Glorious Mystery
Assumption

Bow humbly under God's mighty hand, so in due time he may lift you high. *1 Peter 5:6*

Our Father...

My greetings to Mary, who has worked hard for you. *Romans 16:6*

Hail Mary...

God chose us in him before the world began, to be holy and blameless in his sight, to be full of love... *Ephesians 1:4*

Hail Mary...

We are truly his handiwork, created in Christ Jesus to lead the life of good deeds which God prepared for us in advance. *Ephesians 2:10*

Hail Mary...

Since you have been raised up in company with Christ, set your heart on what pertains to higher realms where Christ is seated at God's right hand. *Colossians 3:1*

Hail Mary...

For if we believe that Jesus died and rose, God will bring forth with him from the dead those also who have fallen asleep believing in him. *1 Thessalonians 4:14*

Hail Mary...

Be intent on things above rather than on things of earth. After all, you have died! Your life is hidden now with Christ in God. *Colossians 3:2-3*

Hail Mary...

His heart embraces you with an expanding love as he recalls the obedience you showed to God when you received him in fear and trembling. *2 Corinthians 7:15*

Hail Mary...

Not all of us shall fall asleep, but all of us are to be changed — in an instant, in the twinkling of an eye, at the sound of the last trumpet. *1 Corinthians 15:51-52*

Hail Mary...

Her good character will be attested to by her good deeds ... Some good deeds stand out clearly as such; even inconspicuous ones cannot be hidden forever. *1 Timothy 5:10,25*

Hail Mary...

Praised be the God and Father of our Lord Jesus Christ, who has bestowed on us in Christ every spiritual blessing in the heavens! *Ephesians 1:3*

Hail Mary...

Glory Be to the Father...

O My Jesus...

Fifth Glorious Mystery
Coronation

Your entry into the everlasting kingdom of our Lord and
Savior Jesus Christ will be richly provided for.
2 Peter 1:11

Our Father...

If our hopes in Christ are limited to this life only, we are
the most pitiable of men. *1 Corinthians 15:19*

Hail Mary...

My entire attention is on the finish line as I run toward
the prize to which God calls me — life on high in Christ
Jesus. *Philippians 3:14*

Hail Mary...

I have fought the good fight, I have finished the race. I
have kept the faith. From now on a merited crown
awaits me ... not only to me, but to all who have looked
for his appearing with eager longing. *2 Timothy 4:7-8*

Hail Mary...

May the God of peace make you perfect in holiness.
May he preserve you whole and entire, spirit, soul and
body. *1 Thessalonians 5:23*

Hail Mary...

"Eye has not seen, ear has not heard, nor has it so much
as dawned on man what God has prepared for those
who love him." *1 Corinthians 2:9*

Hail Mary...

If we have died with him we shall also live with him; If
we hold out to the end we shall also reign with him.
2 Timothy 2:11-12

Hail Mary...

I am sure of this much: that he who has begun the good
work in you will carry it through to completion, right up
to the day of Christ Jesus. *Philippians 1:6*

Hail Mary...

The God of peace will quickly crush Satan under your
feet. *Romans 16:20*

Hail Mary...

When Christ our life appears, then you shall appear with
him in glory. *Colossians 3:4*

Hail Mary...

Imitate me as I imitate Christ. *1 Corinthians 11:1*

Hail Mary...

Glory Be to the Father...

O My Jesus...

Hail Holy Queen...

Shepherd and King

1 Chronicles 11:2, 16:29, Psalms 23:1,
Matthew 1:6, 2:11, Luke 2:1-6, Revelation 12:1,5, 22:16

BOOK SEVEN
Revelation

I know your deeds — your love and faith and service —
as well as your patient endurance; I know also that your
efforts of recent times are greater than ever.
Revelation 2:19

The Our Father Meditation Verses

Selections from Revelation

The Hail Mary Meditation Verses

Selections from Hebrews, James, John, 1 John, 2 John,
3 John, Jude, and Revelation

The Joyful Mysteries

The Sign of the Cross

The Apostle's Creed

We praise you, the Lord God Almighty who is and who was. *Revelation 11:17*

Our Father...

Remember your leaders who spoke the word of God to you; consider how their lives ended, and imitate their faith. *Hebrews 13:7*

Hail Mary for Faith

Beloved, I hope you are in good health — may you thrive in all other ways as you do in the spirit. *3 John 1:2*

Hail Mary for Hope

See what love the Father has bestowed on us in letting us be called children of God! *1 John 3:1*

Hail Mary for Charity

Glory Be to the Father...

O My Jesus...

First Joyful Mystery
Annunciation

The angel said to me: "These words are trustworthy and true; the Lord, the God of prophetic spirits, has sent his angel to show his servant what must happen very soon." *Revelation 22:6*

Our Father...

These are they who believe in his name — who were begotten not by blood, nor by carnal desire, nor by man's willing it, but by God. *John 1:12-13*

Hail Mary...

In the beginning was the Word; the Word was in God's presence, and the Word was God. *John 1:1*

Hail Mary...

Love has no room for fear; rather perfect love casts out all fear. *1 John 4:18*

Hail Mary...

Humbly welcome the word that has taken root in you, with its power to save you. *James 1:21*

Hail Mary...

"Do not let your hearts be troubled. Have faith in God and faith in me." *John 14:1*

Hail Mary...

Faith is confident assurance concerning what we hope for, and conviction about things we do not see. *Hebrews 11:1*

Hail Mary...

If you consider the holiness that is his, you can be sure that everyone who acts in holiness has been begotten by him. *1 John 2:29*

Hail Mary...

Everyone who believes that Jesus is the Christ has been begotten of God. Now, everyone who loves the father loves the child he has begotten. *1 John 5:1*

Hail Mary...

The way we can be sure we are in union with him is for the man who claims to abide in him to conduct himself just as he did. *1 John 2:5-6*

Hail Mary...

God is love. "Live on in me, as I do in you."
1 John 4:8; John 15:4

Hail Mary...

Glory Be to the Father...

O My Jesus...

Second Joyful Mystery
Visitation

The grace of the Lord Jesus be with you all. Amen!
Revelation 22:21

Our Father...

It has given me great joy to find some of your children walking in the path of truth, just as we were commanded by the Father. But now, my Lady ... let us love one another. *2 John 1:4*

Hail Mary...

He who acts in truth comes into the light, to make clear that his deeds are done in God. *John 3:21*

Hail Mary...

Strive for peace with all men, and for that holiness without which no one can see the Lord. *Hebrews 12:14*

Hail Mary...

"My Father has been glorified in your bearing much fruit and becoming my disciples." *John 15:8*

Hail Mary...

You must perceive that a person is justified by his works and not by faith alone. *James 2:24*

Hail Mary...

Beloved, let us love one another because love is of God;
everyone who loves is begotten of God and has
knowledge of God. *1 John 4:7*

Hail Mary...

"I give you a new commandment: Love one another.
Such as my love has been for you, so must your love be
for each other." *John 13:34*

Hail Mary...

There was a man named John sent by God, who came as
a witness to testify to the light, so that through him all
men might believe. *John 1:6-7*

Hail Mary...

He said, quoting the prophet Isaiah, "I am 'a voice in the
desert, crying out: Make straight the way of the Lord!' "
John 1:23

Hail Mary...

John answered them: "I baptize with water. There is one
among you whom you do not recognize — the one who
is to come after me — the strap of whose sandal I am not
worthy to unfasten." *John 1:26-27*

Hail Mary...

Glory Be to the Father...

O My Jesus...

Third Joyful Mystery
Nativity

"It is I, Jesus ... I am the Root and Offspring of David, the Morning Star shining bright." *Revelation 22:16*

Our Father...

She gave birth to a son — a boy destined to shepherd all the nations with an iron rod.
Revelation 12:5

Hail Mary...

"This is God's chosen One." *John 1:34*

Hail Mary...

The Word became flesh and made his dwelling among us, and we have seen his glory: The glory of an only Son coming from the Father, filled with enduring love.
John 1:14

Hail Mary...

He wills to bring us to birth with a word spoken in truth so that we may be a kind of first fruits of his creatures.
James 1:18

Hail Mary...

Indeed, just as the Father possesses life in himself, so has he granted it to the Son to have life in himself.
John 5:26

Hail Mary...

He was in the world, and through him the world was made, yet the world did not know who he was.
John 1:10

Hail Mary...

When anyone acknowledges that Jesus is the Son of God, God dwells in him and he in God. *1 John 4:15*

Hail Mary...

Dearly beloved, we are God's children now; what we shall later be has not come to light. *1 John 3:2*

Hail Mary...

"How can you have seen Abraham?" Jesus answered them: "I solemnly declare it: before Abraham came to be, I AM." *John 8:57-58*

Hail Mary...

The Lord God says, "I am the Alpha and the Omega, the One who is and who was and who is to come, the Almighty!" *Revelation 1:8*

Hail Mary...

Glory Be to the Father...

O My Jesus...

Fourth Joyful Mystery
Presentation

"Praise our God, all you his servants, the small and the great, who revere him!" *Revelation 19:5*

Our Father...

For while the law was given through Moses, this enduring love came through Jesus Christ. *John 1:17*

Hail Mary...

"I have come to the world as its light, to keep anyone who believes in me from remaining in the dark." *John 12:46*

Hail Mary...

Let what you heard from the beginning remain in your hearts. *1 John 2:24*

Hail Mary...

The woman said to him: "I know there is a Messiah coming ... When he comes, he will tell us everything." Jesus replied, "I who speak to you am he." *John 4:25-26*

Hail Mary...

"I came forth from God, and am here." *John 8:42*

Hail Mary...

"It is not to do my own will that I have come down from heaven, but to do the will of him who sent me."
John 6:38

Hail Mary...

"I have come to do your will." In other words, he takes away the first covenant to establish the second.
Hebrews 10:9

Hail Mary...

"The works I do in my Father's name give witness in my favor..." *John 10:25*

Hail Mary...

Christ was faithful as the Son placed over God's house.
Hebrews 3:6

Hail Mary...

The Jews responded, "What sign can you show us authorizing you to do these things?" "Destroy this temple," was Jesus' answer, "and in three days I will raise it up." *John 2:18-19*

Hail Mary...

Glory Be to the Father...

O My Jesus...

Fifth Joyful Mystery
Finding in the Temple

I also saw a new Jerusalem, the holy city ... I heard a loud voice from the throne cry out: "This is God's dwelling among men. He shall dwell with them and they shall be his people and he shall be their God who is always with them..." *Revelation 21:2-3*

Our Father...

Jesus went out to the Mount of Olives. At daybreak he reappeared in the temple area; and when the people started coming to him, he sat down and began to teach them. *John 8:1-2*

Hail Mary...

This Son is the reflection of the Father's glory, the exact representation of the Father's being, and he sustains all things by his powerful word. *Hebrews 1:3*

Hail Mary...

"Rabbi," he said, "we know you are a teacher come from God, for no man can perform signs and wonders such as you perform unless God is with him." *John 3:2*

Hail Mary...

"You address me as 'Teacher' and 'Lord,' and fittingly enough, for that is what I am." *John 13:13*

Hail Mary...

Anyone who remains rooted in the teaching possesses both the Father and the Son. *2 John 1:9*

Hail Mary...

Even Christ did not glorify himself with the office of high priest; he received it from the One who said to him, "You are my son; today I have begotten you."
Hebrews 5:5

Hail Mary...

"I am the good shepherd. I know my sheep and my sheep know me..." *John 10:14*

Hail Mary...

Jesus performed this first of his signs at Cana in Galilee. Thus did he reveal his glory, and his disciples believed in him. *John 2:11*

Hail Mary...

When the people saw the sign he performed they began to say, "This is undoubtedly the Prophet who is to come into the world." *John 6:14*

Hail Mary...

The Pharisees called a meeting of the Sanhedrin. "What are we to do," they said, "with this man performing all sorts of signs? If we let him go on like this, the whole world will believe in him." *John 11:47*

Hail Mary...

Glory Be to the Father...

O My Jesus...

Hail Holy Queen....

The Sorrowful Mysteries

The Sign of the Cross

The Apostle's Creed

"How long will it be, O Master, holy and true, before you judge our cause and avenge our blood among the inhabitants of the earth?" *Revelation 6:10*

Our Father...

My brothers, what good is it to profess faith without practicing it? *James 2:14*

Hail Mary for Faith

Those who have endured we call blessed. *James 5:11*

Hail Mary for Hope

I ask you, how can God's love survive in a man who has enough of this world's goods yet closes his heart to his brother when he sees him in need? *1 John 3:17*

Hail Mary for Charity

Glory Be to the Father...

O My Jesus...

First Sorrowful Mystery
Agony in the Garden

I will keep you safe in the time of trial which is coming on the whole world, to test all men on earth. *Revelation 3:10*

> *Our Father...*

Jesus grew deeply troubled. He went on to give this testimony: "I tell you solemnly, one of you will betray me." *John 13:21*

> *Hail Mary...*

If anyone among you is suffering hardship, he must pray. *James 5:13*

> *Hail Mary...*

Jesus went out with disciples across the Kidron Valley. There was a garden there, and he and his disciples entered it. *John 18:1*

> *Hail Mary...*

In the days when he was in the flesh, he offered prayers and supplications with loud cries and tears to God ... Son though he was, he learned obedience from what he suffered... *Hebrews 5:7-8*

> *Hail Mary...*

Judas took the cohort as well as guards supplied by the chief priest and the Pharisees, and came there with lanterns, torches and weapons. Jesus, aware of all that would happen to him, stepped forward. *John 18:3-4*

> *Hail Mary...*

Jesus ... said to them. "Who is it you want?" "Jesus the
Nazorean," they replied, "I am he," he answered.
John 18:4-5

Hail Mary...

Then Simon Peter, who had a sword, drew it and struck
the slave of the high priest, severing his right ear.
John 18:10

Hail Mary...

At that Jesus said to Peter, "Put your sword back in its
sheath. Am I not to drink the cup the Father has given
me?" *John 18:11*

Hail Mary...

We have this confidence in God: that he hears us
whenever we ask for anything according to his will.
1 John 5:14

Hail Mary...

Then the soldiers of the cohort, their tribune, and the
Jewish guards arrested Jesus and bound him.
John 18:12

Hail Mary...

Glory Be to the Father...

O My Jesus...

Second Sorrowful Mystery
Scourging

To him who loves us and freed us from our sins by his own blood. *Revelation 1:5*

Our Father...

Pilate went back into the praetorium and summoned Jesus. "Are you the King of the Jews?" *John 18:33*

Hail Mary...

My brothers, count it pure joy when you are involved in every sort of trial. Realize that when your faith is tested this makes for endurance. *James 1:2-3*

Hail Mary...

Jesus answered, "Are you saying this on your own, or have others been telling you about me?" *John 18:34*

Hail Mary...

"I am no Jew!" Pilate retorted. "It is your own people and the chief priests who have handed you over to me. What have you done?" *John 18:35*

Hail Mary...

Jesus answered: "My kingdom does not belong to this world." *John 18:36*

Hail Mary...

"If my kingdom were of this world, my subjects would be fighting to save me from being handed over to the Jews." *John 18:36*

Hail Mary...

"As it is my kingdom is not here." At this Pilate said to him, "So, then, you are a king?" *John 18:36-37*

Hail Mary...

Jesus replied: "It is you who say I am a king. The reason I was born, the reason why I came into the world, is to testify to the truth. Anyone committed to the truth hears my voice." *John 18:37*

Hail Mary...

In truth and love, then, we shall have grace, mercy, and peace from God the Father and from Jesus Christ, the Father's Son. *2 John 1:3*

Hail Mary...

Pilate's next move was to take Jesus and have him scourged. *John 19:1*

Hail Mary...

Glory Be to the Father...

O My Jesus...

Third Sorrowful Mystery
Crowning with Thorns

If one is destined to be slain by the sword, by the sword he will be slain! Such is the faithful endurance that distinguishes God's holy people. *Revelation 13:10*

Our Father...

You need patience to do God's will and receive what he has promised. *Hebrews 10:36*

Hail Mary...

The soldiers then wove a crown of thorns and fixed it on his head, throwing around his shoulders a cloak of royal purple. *John 19:2*

Hail Mary...

He wore a cloak that had been dipped in blood, and his name was the Word of God. *Revelation 19:13*

Hail Mary...

According to the law almost everything is purified by blood, and without the shedding of blood there is no forgiveness. *Hebrews 9:22*

Hail Mary...

Repeatedly they came up to him and said, "All hail, king of the Jews!" slapping his face as they did so. *John 19:3*

Hail Mary...

A name was written on the part of the cloak that covered his thigh: "King of kings and Lord of lords."
Revelation 19:16

Hail Mary...

When Jesus came out wearing the crown of thorns and the purple cloak, Pilate said to them "Look at the man!" They shouted, "Crucify him! Crucify him!" *John 19:5-6*

Hail Mary...

Pilate asked him. "Do you not know that I have the power to release you and the power to crucify you?" *John 19:10*

Hail Mary...

Jesus answered: "You would have no power over me whatever unless it were given you from above." *John 19:11*

Hail Mary...

Pilate exclaimed, "Shall I crucify your king?" The chief priests replied, "We have no king but Caesar." *John 19:15*

Hail Mary...

Glory Be to the Father...

O My Jesus...

Fourth Sorrowful Mystery
Carrying of the Cross

Have no fear of the sufferings to come. *Revelation 2:10*

Our Father...

In the end, Pilate handed Jesus over to be crucified. Jesus was led away. *John 19:16*

Hail Mary...

"If anyone would serve me, let him follow me; where I am, there will my servant be. *John 12:26*

Hail Mary...

And carrying the cross by himself, [Jesus] went out to what is called the Place of the Skull. *John 19:17*

Hail Mary...

There is One who can protect you from a fall and make you stand unblemished and exultant in the presence of his glory. *Jude 1:24*

Hail Mary...

I know your deeds, your labors, and your patient endurance ... You are patient and endure hardship for my cause. *Revelation 2:2-3*

Hail Mary...

Endure your trials as the discipline of God, who deals with you as sons. *Hebrews 12:7*

Hail Mary...

"I tell you truly: you will weep and mourn while the world rejoices; you will grieve for a time, but your grief will be turned into joy." *John 16:20*

Hail Mary...

You, too, must be patient ... you have heard of the steadfastness of Job, and have seen what the Lord, who is compassionate and merciful, did in the end. *James 5:8,11*

Hail Mary...

"The Father loves me for this: that I lay down my life to take it up again. No one takes it from me; I lay it down freely." *John 10:17-18*

Hail Mary...

Love then, consists in this: not that we have loved God, but that he has loved us and has sent his Son as an offering for our sins. *1 John 4:10*

Hail Mary...

Glory Be to the Father...

O My Jesus...

Fifth Sorrowful Mystery
Crucifixion

This is the new hymn they sang: "Worthy are you to receive the scroll and break open its seals, for you were slain. With your blood you purchased for God men of every race and tongue, of every people and nation."
Revelation 5:9

Our Father...

There they crucified him, and two others with him: one on either side, Jesus in the middle. *John 19:18*

Hail Mary...

Pilate had an inscription placed on the cross which read,
JESUS THE NAZOREAN
THE KING OF THE JEWS.

John 19:19

Hail Mary...

Near the cross of Jesus there stood his mother, his mother's sister, Mary the wife of Clopas, and Mary Magdalene. *John 19:25*

Hail Mary...

Seeing his mother there with the disciple whom he loved, Jesus said to his mother, "Woman, there is your son." In turn he said to the disciple, "There is your mother." *John 19:26-27*

Hail Mary...

Jesus realizing that everything was now finished, said to fulfill the Scripture, "I am thirsty." *John 19:28*

Hail Mary...

When Jesus took the wine, he said, "Now it is finished." Then he bowed his head, and delivered over his spirit. *John 19:30*

Hail Mary...

"There is the Lamb of God who takes away the sin of the world!" *John 1:29*

Hail Mary...

He had to become like his brothers in every way, that he might be a merciful and faithful high priest before God on their behalf, to expiate the sins of the people. *Hebrews 2:17*

Hail Mary...

He is an offering for our sins, and not for our sins only, but for those of the whole world. *1 John 2:2*

Hail Mary...

"Yes, God so loved the world that he gave his only Son, that whoever believes in him may not die but may have eternal life." *John 3:16*

Hail Mary...

Glory Be to the Father...

O My Jesus...

Hail Holy Queen...

The Glorious Mysteries

The Sign of the Cross

The Apostle's Creed

"O Lord our God, you are worthy to receive glory and honor and power! For you have created all things; by your will they came to be and were made!"
Revelation 4:11

Our Father...

The throne of God and of the Lamb shall be there, and his servants shall serve him faithfully. *Revelation 22:3*

Hail Mary for Faith

Everyone who has this hope based on him keeps himself pure, as he is pure. *1 John 3:3*

Hail Mary for Hope

Persevere in God's love, and welcome the mercy of our Lord Jesus Christ which leads to life eternal. *Jude 1:21*

Hail Mary for Charity

Glory Be to the Father...

O My Jesus...

First Glorious Mystery
Resurrection

I am the First and the Last and the One who lives. Once I was dead but now I live — forever and ever. I hold the keys of death and the nether world. *Revelation 1:17-18*

Our Father...

They took Jesus' body, and in accordance with Jewish burial custom bound it up in wrappings of cloth with perfumed oils. *John 19:40*

Hail Mary...

They retorted, "This temple took forty-six years to build, and you are going to 'raise it up in three days'!" Actually he was talking about the temple of his body.
John 2:20-21

Hail Mary...

Early in the morning on the first day of the week, while it was still dark, Mary Magdalene came to the tomb.
John 20:1

Hail Mary...

Mary stood weeping beside the tomb ... she turned around and caught sight of Jesus standing there. But she did not know him. *John 20:11,14*

Hail Mary...

"Woman," he asked her, "why are you weeping? Who is it you are looking for?" ... Jesus said to her, "Mary!" ... Mary Magdalene went to the disciples. "I have seen the Lord!" *John 20:15-16,18*

Hail Mary...

No one has gone up to heaven except the One who came down from there — the Son of Man... *John 3:13*

Hail Mary...

Just as Moses lifted up the serpent in the desert, so must the Son of Man be lifted up that all who believe may have eternal life in him. *John 3:14-15*

Hail Mary...

Jesus came and stood before them. "Peace be with you," he said; then to Thomas: "Take your finger and examine my hands. Put your hand into my side." *John 20:26-27*

Hail Mary...

Thomas said in response, "My Lord and my God!" Jesus then said to him: "You became a believer because you saw me. Blest are they who have not seen and have believed." *John 20:28-29*

Hail Mary...

He who feeds on my flesh and drinks my blood has life eternal, and I will raise him on the last day. *John 6:54*

Hail Mary...

Glory Be to the Father...

O My Jesus...

Second Glorious Mystery
Ascension

See, he comes amid the clouds! Every eye shall see him, even of those who pierced him. *Revelation 1:7*

Our Father...

Jesus then said: "Do not cling to me, for I have not yet ascended to the Father. Rather, go to my brothers and tell them 'I am ascending to my Father and your Father, to my God and your God!'" *John 20:17*

Hail Mary...

"Worthy is the Lamb that was slain to receive power and riches, wisdom and strength, honor and glory and praise!" *Revelation 5:12*

Hail Mary...

Jesus then said to them: "Only a little while longer am I to be with you, then I am going away to him who sent me. You will look for me, but you will not find me; where I am you cannot come." *John 7:33-34*

Hail Mary...

Her child was caught up to God and to his throne. *Revelation 12:5*

Hail Mary...

He is always able to save those who approach God through him, since he forever lives to make intercession for them. *Hebrews 7:25*

Hail Mary...

"Did I not assure you that if you believed you would see the glory of God displayed?" *John 11:40*

Hail Mary...

"To the One seated on the throne, and to the Lamb, be praise and honor, glory and might, forever and ever!" *Revelation 5:13*

Hail Mary...

Christ was offered up once to take away the sins of many; he will appear a second time not to take away sin but to bring salvation to those who eagerly await him. *Hebrews 9:28*

Hail Mary...

The One who gives this testimony says, "Yes, I am coming soon!" Amen! Come, Lord, Jesus! *Revelation 22:20*

Hail Mary...

Holy, holy, holy, is the Lord God Almighty, He who was, and who is, and who is to come! *Revelation 4:8*

Hail Mary...

Glory Be to the Father...

O My Jesus...

Third Glorious Mystery
Descent of the Holy Spirit

Let him who has ears heed the Spirit's word to the churches! *Revelation 2:7 [2:11, 2:17, 2:29, 3:6, 3:13, 3:22]*

Our Father...

Every worthwhile gift, every genuine benefit comes from above, descending from the Father of the heavenly luminaries... *James 1:17*

Hail Mary...

"It is much better for you that I go. If I fail to go, the Paraclete will never come to you, whereas if I go, I will send him to you." *John 16:7*

Hail Mary...

Wherefore, we who are receiving the unshakable kingdom should hold fast to God's grace, through which we may offer worship acceptable to him in reverence and awe. For our God is a consuming fire. *Hebrews 12:28-29*

Hail Mary...

The Paraclete, the Holy Spirit whom the Father will send in my name, will instruct you in everything, and remind you of all that I told you. *John 14:26*

Hail Mary...

This is how you can recognize God's Spirit: every spirit that acknowledges Jesus Christ come in the flesh belongs to God... *1 John 4:2*

Hail Mary...

"I solemnly assure you, no one can enter God's kingdom without being begotten of water and Spirit." *John 3:5*

Hail Mary...

This is how we know that he remains in us: from the Spirit that he gave us. *1 John 3:24*

Hail Mary...

Spirit begets spirit. *John 3:6*

Hail Mary...

It is the spirit that gives life... *John 6:63*

Hail Mary...

Beloved, grow strong in your holy faith through prayer in the Holy Spirit. *Jude 1:20*

Hail Mary...

Glory Be to the Father...

O My Jesus...

Fourth Glorious Mystery
Assumption

So rejoice, you heavens, and you that dwell therein!
Revelation 12:12

> Our Father...

"I am the gate. Whoever enters through me will be safe."
John 10:9

> Hail Mary...

Our love is brought to perfection in this, that we should
have confidence on the day of judgment; for our relation
to this world is just like his. *1 John 4:17*

> Hail Mary...

Time to reward your servants the prophets and the holy
ones who revere you, the great and the small alike.
Revelation 11:18

> Hail Mary...

"I solemnly assure you, the man who hears my word and
has faith in him who sent me possesses eternal life."
John 5:24

> Hail Mary...

Whoever keeps his word, truly has the love of God been
made perfect in him. *1 John 2:5*

> Hail Mary...

Each person was judged according to his conduct.
Revelation 20:13

> Hail Mary...

He himself made us a promise and the promise is no less
than this: eternal life. *1 John 2:25*

Hail Mary...

"I am the resurrection and the life; whoever believes in
me, though he should die, will come to life; and whoever
is alive and believes in me will never die." *John 11:25-26*

Hail Mary...

Whoever does what is good belongs to God...
3 John 1:11

Hail Mary...

The grace of the Lord Jesus be with you all. Amen!
Revelation 22:21

Hail Mary...

Glory Be to the Father...

O My Jesus...

Fifth Glorious Mystery
Coronation

A great sign appeared in the sky, a woman clothed with the sun, with the moon under her feet, and on her head a crown of twelve stars. *Revelation 12:1*

Our Father...

Happy the man who holds out to the end through trial! Once he has been proved, he will receive the crown of life the Lord has promised to those who love him. *James 1:12*

Hail Mary...

The man who does God's will endures forever. *1 John 2:17*

Hail Mary...

"I solemnly assure you, he who accepts anyone I send accepts me, and in accepting me accepts him who sent me." *John 13:20*

Hail Mary...

Those who keep his commandments remain in him and he in them. *1 John 3:24*

Hail Mary...

If what you heard from the beginning does remain in your hearts, then you in turn will remain in the Son and in the Father. *1 John 2:24*

Hail Mary...

"If anyone serves me, him the Father will honor." *John 12:26*

Hail Mary...

"I am indeed going to prepare a place for you, and then I shall come back to take you with me, that where I am you also may be." *John 14:3*

Hail Mary...

Remain faithful until death and I will give you the crown of life. *Revelation 2:10*

Hail Mary...

Imitate those who, through faith and patience, are inheriting the promises. *Hebrews 6:12*

Hail Mary...

Alleluia! The Lord is King, our God, the Almighty! Let us rejoice and be glad, and give him glory!
Revelation 19:6-7

Hail Mary...

Glory Be to the Father...

O My Jesus...

Hail Holy Queen...

I have given you glory on earth by finishing the work you gave me to do. *John 17:4*